STROKE

THE INSIDE STORY OF OLYMPIC CONTENDERS

STROKE

HEATHER CLARKE AND SUSAN GWYNNE-TIMOTHY

James Lorimer & Company, Publishers
Toronto 1988

Front cover photograph: Andrei Grushman
Back cover photographs: Hardolph Wasteneys

Canadian Cataloguing in Publication Data
Clarke, Heather
Stroke: the inside story of Olympic contenders
ISBN 1-55028-037-6 (bound) ISBN 1-55028-035-X (pbk.)
1. Rowers - Canada - Biography. 2. Women athletes - Canada -
Biography. 3. Rowing - Canada. I. Gwynne-Timothy, Susan.
II. Title.
GV790.9.C58 1988   797.1'23'0922   C88-093676-2

James Lorimer & Company, Publishers
Egerton Ryerson Memorial Building
35 Britain Street
Toronto, Ontario M5A 1R7
Printed and bound in Canada
5 4 3 2 1   88 89 90 91 92 93

Contents

This book is dedicated to Norma Clarke
and Sylvia Gwynne-Timothy

Acknowledgments

We would like to thank our editor, Heather Robertson, for giving two novices a crash course on how to write a book over the fall and winter of 1987-88. We would also like to thank the Explorations Program of the Canada Council for awarding us the grant that enabled us to undertake the project.

Our gratitude goes to our many friends, family members, fellow athletes, coaches and associates, without whose contributions and encouragement we would never have written this book: Barb Armbrust, Kathryn Barr, Rob Beamish, Stephen Beatty, Jan Borowy, Doug Clark, Pauline and Tina Clarke, Joy Fera, Diana, Gordon and Jack Gwynne-Timothy, Doug Hamilton, Drew Harrison, Catherine Harry, Heather Hattin, Jim Joy, Barb Kirch, Silken Laumann, Kathy Lichty, Carol Love, Cathy Lund, Peter MacGowan, Grant Main, Archie and Barbara Mallock, Anne and Betsy Marden, Ian McFarlane, Kevin Neufeld, Sarah Ogilvie, the Olympic Academy of Canada, Gary Owens, Carla Pace, Valeria Recila, George Rawlyk, Lisa Robertson, Ian Robson, Bill Rowell, Angie Schneider, Andrea Schreiner, Tricia Smith, Nancy Storrs, Lesley Thompson, Jane Tregunno, Stephen van Gronigen, Jenny Walinga, Tracey Walt, Hardolph Wasteneys, Rudy Wieler, Kay Worthington. We also wish to thank John Partington and Terry Orlick for permitting us to use material from their book *Psyched*.

PROLOGUE: ATALANTA SPEAKS

Atalanta was the beautiful daughter of a king. Raised in the wilderness, she became a famous huntress. She did not want to get married, although she had many suitors. She said she would only marry the man who could beat her in a running race. But if she won, her opponent would die. Many men challenged her and died. Unathletic Hippomenes loved her truly but knew he could not beat her in a race. So he prayed to Aphrodite to give him aid.

Aphrodite gave him three golden apples.

As Atalanta drew ahead in the race against Hippomenes, he threw down the first apple. The apple signified the awareness of passing time. Atalanta picked it up. Startled, she saw her face in it, as it would be when she grew old. But she kept on running. As she passed Hippomenes, he threw down the second apple. Atalanta picked it up, too. It represented the importance of love, which until then Atalanta had scorned. She hesitated in her stride. But the finish line was in sight. She was about to cross it, ahead of Hippomenes, when he threw down the third apple. That apple symbolized creativity and the procreative instinct. Atalanta was not going to pick it up, but glanced down to look at it. Then she stooped to pick up that apple, too. As she did so, Hippomenes passed her, won the race and claimed her for his bride.

Our book is the story of eight modern-day Atalantas: Heather Clarke, Tina Clarke, Silken Laumann, Lisa Robertson, Andrea Schreiner, Tricia Smith, Jane Tregunno and Kay Worthington. They carry the encumbering golden apples of adult awareness, but perform anyway. Their belief in the Olympic dream is buttressed with a disabused awareness of what it takes to make it come true. Their experience has made them strong.

In this book the eight oarswomen talk about being women in sport as they prepare for the Olympic Games of 1988. Performance demands autonomy and commitment. Atalanta was assertive, goal oriented, self-assured and competitive before she was distracted by the golden apples. Yet, in losing, she "achieved" the feminine ideal of connection, that is, marriage. In the legend, Atalanta did not speak up to say how she felt, gaining the one at the expense of the other. But she speaks up in our book, through the lives of eight women who want to have it all.

INTRODUCTION

Much has been written about Olympic athletes, but little has been written by them about what they really feel and believe behind the hype of the media. This book is the story of eight oarswomen on the Canadian Olympic team, told from their point of view. It is based on extensive interviews with the women, plus interviews with twenty-five coaches and other athletes, conducted during the months leading up to the 1988 Seoul Olympic Games.

This book tells why rowers love to row. Why they get up in the grey dawn and creep outside when the rest of the world is asleep. Rowers love to glide through the mist with no sound but the catch-push of the oars hooking into the water. They love the physical feel of the oar, their muscles, the water bubbling under the hull. Being outside with the elements, the wind, the sunrise or the rain. It feels so good, too, to move as one with all the others in the crew, focusing every ounce of energy to push like hell yet blend in harmony. Executing the stroke in synchrony demands utter concentration from everyone in the boat. It is relaxing and exhausting at the same instant.

This book also looks at the nature of crew rowing. Pierre de Coubertin, who founded the modern Olympic movement in 1896, observed that crew rowing is the ultimate team sport. All the team members are "in the same boat," which will perform only as well as their perfectly coordinated effort makes it. The Olympic final is won by the best crew, regardless of the individual excellence of any one athlete in the field of boats. The athletes in a crew must compete fiercely against one another to make it, and then they have to pull together in a race. Thus, rowers synthesize the two opposing demands of interdependency and self-reliance. As teammates, they get to know each other's strengths and vulnerabilities. They develop respect and trust for each other, and create the corporate identity of the crew.

What does it mean to be an Olympic competitor? Racing at the Olympic level means taking up the personal challenge to be tougher mentally than everyone else, to train longer, work harder. It is forcing the mind's will on the body when the body cannot give anymore. The personal challenge means that when two athletes find themselves evenly matched in the race, the one who can stand more pain wins. Rowers are snobs about the amount of pain they endure and the training they do to be good. They respect their teammates because they know how much they have sacrificed in time and energy to be where they are.

Questions are still asked about the appropriateness of women rowing. Competitive rowers must be strong, tough, aggressive — typically masculine qualities. Successful oarswomen have those characteristics — yet those qualities go against traditional ideas of femininity. Oarswomen have discovered over the years that society has contradictory expectations of them in the two roles of female and athlete. The women on the 1988 team have worked at synthesizing the two in their efforts to live full lives over their years of national team competition. We will point out how the oarswomen as individuals have balanced the two roles. We make no general conclusions about women in sport and have not consulted any of the scholarly writing that exists on the subject.

Women are latecomers (1976 Olympics) to rowing and are still finding their own niche in the sport. Women cannot fit the traditional rowing image of "elite and male," which has been hallowed by rowing's 150 years as a college sport. Like other women who want to work hard and be successful in non-traditional environments, the oarswomen have had to construct their own place.

We, the two co-authors of this book, started rowing under coaches who believed in our potential and were able to communicate their passion for rowing to us. For us, the dream became the reality of serious competition. Heather, who is one of the eight oarswomen in the book, made her first national team in 1979. Susan rowed on the junior national team in 1980; she retired from the sport in 1985 after rowing on the national development team. The reality of the national team understandably differed from our expectations. Being from strong and sheltered families, we had to adjust to new values in the competitive and tough-minded environment of sport. We dealt with new measures of success and new standards of social conformity. Despite our initial reservations, rowing culture and our friends there shaped our values. We developed the desire for excellence with rowing as the means. We wanted acceptance by those who also struggled for excellence. We were hooked.

Over the years, we listened to other rowers tell and retell their rowing stories, and we told and retold our own. The stories are a folk memory. In the academic year of 1986-87, Heather worked on a research project at Queen's University that looked at the status of all national team athletes in Canada. We realized then that our experience in rowing expresses some issues of wider interest to athletes, to those interested in Olympic athletes and to anyone who dreams dreams and tries to make them reality.

As intense young adults, the oarswomen training for 1988 have lived a rich variety of experiences over the years. Together as teammates they have made sense of tragedies and triumphs. In the book we will describe some of the landmark events in this team's development. These oarswomen are contenders for Olympic medals. They are wading through sloughs of despond, dashing triumphantly along sunlit hillsides, killing dragons and giving themselves pep talks as they train for the Seoul Olympics in South Korea in September 1988.

1

ON TRACK

At 4 p.m. on July 31, 1987, the five members of the Canadian women's coxed four (four oarswomen with coxswain) lined up beside their rowing shell in the boathouse bay at Burnaby Lake near Vancouver. They had come over from Victoria to race the women's pair, Tricia Smith and Betty Craig, who had won the silver at the 1984 Olympics. The four looked forward to tough racing against them. In this practice race, the coxed four, being a faster boat than the pair, would start twenty seconds behind, to make it a race for the finish.

"On the boat!" called Lesley Thompson, the coxswain.

At five feet two inches, Lesley provided a striking contrast to the women in her crew. Three of them were over six feet tall; Heather Clarke, the fourth, stood five feet nine inches. Two to a side, the women lifted the forty-five-foot shell to their shoulders. Heather stood on her tiptoes to share the 125-pound weight with the others. They walked from the dimness of the boat bay into the hot afternoon sun. At the bottom of the sloping dock they stopped.

"Over the heads, ready, press!" commanded Lesley.

In one graceful motion the four women pushed the yellow carbonfibre boat over their heads. They did a half turn, bent together and lowered the boat to the water. Kathryn Barr in the bow seat and Jane Tregunno, rowing stroke in the stern, held the fragile boat so that the waves wouldn't push it against the dock. Heather Clarke and Jenny Walinga brought the four oars over and secured them in the oarlocks. Meanwhile, Lesley attached her coxbox — the speaker system through which she spoke to the crew — into her perch. She lay full-length in the bow, forward of Kathryn's back, wedged in by pieces of styrofoam to prevent her from slipping out of sight. She was the eyes of the boat, the only one who faced the finish line.

"One foot in, and down!" said Lesley. The women sat down and pushed the boat out. They had to lean away from the dock to continue the outward momentum of the boat. The waves washed over the gunwhales on the windward side. Lesley swore as the green slime hit her face. "Careful, you guys!" she complained, suddenly human. Lesley is a little dynamo, with her gymnast's physique and fierce competitiveness. Outburst over, she instantly resumed her role of ritual formality. "Full crew ready? Row!"

This afternoon's workout was to be a one-shot deal — one 2,000-metre race. Although it was a shorter workout than most, it was more intense, for the coxed four had the added push of competition against the pair. Or so they thought. Unfortunately, Tricia and Betty tipped during the warm-up when another crew, unfamiliar with the course, crashed into them. Over they went, angry and helpless, landing in the murky water. Betty hurt her back, and the pair cancelled out of the day's practice.

So the coxed four were left to race the clock. The additional irony was that they had come to Burnaby for calm water. On Elk Lake, where they trained in Victoria, they dodged waterskiers. But today there was a vicious headwind, and the day before a tornado had hit one end of the lake.

"Êtes-vous prêt?" called the coach, Drew Harrison, using the French starting command for international rowing races. The women in the four sat motionless, expectant. But inside they churned with pent-up energy. "Oh shoot!" thought Jane. "Why does starting even a practice race make me have to pee?" The adrenalin will do it every time.

"Partez!"

The boat leaped forward. Four pairs of legs drove down like pistons firing in an engine. Four pairs of lean tanned arms pulled their oars in and then pushed them away from their bodies. The secret of crew rowing is for the crew to move as one, repeating each stroke perfectly. The women's feet, fastened in running shoes on angled boards — the footstops — were the only part of their bodies that stayed put during the stroke. The oars pivoted, the sliding seats moved back and forth on their metal tracks. Casual observers would have missed the aggression in the women's rowing. They would have noticed rather the elegance of the athletes swinging in graceful rhythm, the boat on the gold-blue water with the mountains as backdrop. The water sparkled and splashed as the oars reached back to hook it, and the women drove their muscular legs down again. And again. Two hundred strokes into the race Lesley barked, "We've got to go NOW. Build for the finish."

In stroke seat, Jane knifed her blade more savagely into the water. Heather, rowing behind her in three seat, thought of seizing the water before it swirled by. "The stroke rate has to come up." Lesley's voice was insistent. Heather tried to force the cadence up herself, to get a bit more out of the boat by straining against it. Then she reminded herself that it worked when she relaxed into the rhythm. Let the shell glide. Feel the run. Listen for the air bubbles rushing under the hull. Push. With her body flushing with the waves of lactic acid, relaxing didn't come easily. But the stroke rate per minute went up half a beat.

"I want more. Take it up again, over three," said Lesley. They were still rowing too low for a sprint finish. Panic rose in Heather's throat but she gulped it down. "Wind it, Jane," she croaked.

Jane's arms pumped into her body and around the finish of the stroke. Heather knew that Jane would attack, but wanted her to know that the rest of the crew would help her. Jenny in two seat and Kathryn in bow — they wanted it! Together the crew forced their blades into the water just that much quicker, through and out and around more aggressively. For the major international race before the World Championships, the 1987 Rotsee Regatta in Lucerne, Switzerland, they had come up with the motto "Take it together" and had won a silver. The motto was too cutesy for Heather, although she had coined the phrase. Tongue-in-cheek, she called it "the big TIT."

Yet togetherness was the essence of rowing a crew boat. Every member of the coxed four had to take responsibility for the sprint. The rating went up another beat to thirty-six strokes a minute. But in the headwind nothing seemed to happen. Where was the finish line? The crew struggled to control their bodies, whipped by the wind and water. They were weaving with exhaustion when the boat finally crossed the line.

"Let 'er run. Good work," called Lesley. The oars drifted with the water as the athletes gave in to their pain. After a race, even just a practice, no one can sit down, breathe comfortably or think coherently. But the pain is what they discipline themselves to take. Red-hot pokers burning their throats, blood hammering in their heads, they clung to the gunwhales of the boat in an effort to lift their hips out of the seats. The blades, forgotten, pivoted in the oarlocks and caught the water backwards. A portside oar churned up a mess of lily pads. The putrid odour upset Jane's post-race stomach. She leaned over her oar. Heather reached forward to pat Jane's shoulder.

"We can do it," thought Heather. It was such a rush to feel that excitement, even through the haze of pain.

Drew called through his megaphone: "Do a four-kilometre warm-down, and then row in to the dock."

Twenty minutes later, the four glided the last few metres to the dock. The women hitched the starboard side high out of the water so that the oars would rest on the low dock. The narrow shell came to a stop. The women each balanced one foot on the crosspiece between the slide tracks, raised themselves from their seats and stepped out portside, pulling their oars across the boat.

They were training that day, that summer, for the 1987 World Championships in Copenhagen. The 2,000-metre coxed four race takes approximately 250 strokes and is six minutes and forty-five seconds long for world champions in optimal conditions. In rowing, times actually mean little, because wind and water conditions vary so much. With the headwind and the silty water in Burnaby, the race that afternoon had taken the crew almost eight minutes.

But perhaps the severe conditions foreshadowed the four's race a month later in Copenhagen. The crew was expecting a dogfight for bronze at the 1987 Worlds with the Russians, Bulgarians and Americans. The Canadian oarswomen hoped to be with the leaders, the Romanians and the East Germans. Although the crew's composition had changed each year, its performance had been consistently good. They won a silver medal in the 1984 Olympics and bronzes in the 1985 and 1986 World Championships. Unfortunately, in 1987 the Canadians drew a lane that was particularly open to the strong cross headwind. Like all the crews in lane one that day, they finished the final in sixth place.

The 1987 Championships were part of the buildup for the four-year goal of the Seoul Olympics in 1988. Had they won a medal, the coxed four would have qualified automatically for Seoul. But when they didn't and neither did any of the other Canadian women's crews except the single sculler, the question of selection for the Canadian Olympic team was opened up. Canada wants to put together one boat that will win a gold medal. That takes strategic planning — determining where the Canadian team's own strength lies and where the international competition is. The Canadian talent pool is such that, based on the oarswomen's past performances, the eight is guaranteed an Olympic entry. After 1987's disappointing results, a four and a pair could only qualify for Seoul by coming in the top half of the field at Lucerne in July 1988.

In January 1988, twenty-four women were selected to try out for Olympic crews: sixteen plus two coxswains to row sweep — with one oar — and six for the sculling team, to row with two smaller oars. The athletes are named to their particular crews in March and May. But the Olympic team itself, except for the single and the eight, isn't confirmed until July. It's a long time to be on the edge.

Athletes feel particularly on the edge during selection camps. The March 1988 selection camp at Elk Lake in Victoria was extremely important because the eight, the top sweep crew, was to be selected there. The oarswomen rowed together and raced in different combinations over the two weeks. To start off the racing at the beginning of the camp, the veteran oarswomen competed against each other. The up-and-coming oarswomen also competed among themselves. Later, the best of the new raced against the slower of the more experienced athletes.

After three hours on the lake in the sleet, the women competing for the 1988 team docked the boats they had been in for that morning's three races. Their hands had been so cold during the pre-race warm-up that they'd had to stop to tuck them in their armpits. The blood had painfully returned, and they had regained enough feeling in their hands to manipulate the wooden oar handles. Later, during the races, they worked so hard they sweated through their warm woolen layers and had to shed many of them.

Now, the races over for the day, the athletes were chilled. They hurried to put away their boats. One of the single scullers tied her sodden sweatshirts around her waist. She had piled them one by one in the bottom of her single during her workout. They were too wet to wear after sopping up all the water that had splashed into the boat. She undid the oars from her oarlocks, placed them together on the ground and swung the twenty-six-pound, twenty-five-foot boat onto her head. Like an African bearer, she held it there with one hand while dipping down to gather up her oars with the other. But two blades are just a little more than a handful. They almost slipped out of her grasp as she trudged up the dock to the bay, trying to balance them and the boat too.

It was a relief to pass from the wet and wind into the dark, sheltered boat bay, although for a moment the athletes could not see anything. They put their boats and blades away by feel, and then, their eyes adjusted, they huddled together putting on warm clothes. Then they filled their water bottles from the tap on the wall. Together they stretched, to get the knots and cricks out of well-defined muscles. They were equals in their fatigue. But the athletes knew that in a few moments Drew would call them over and announce the outcome of that first round of racing. The pecking order had begun. They nervously laughed and teased as they waited. The athletes were glad to be back together again after training in their own environs during the winter months. But they would be more at ease with each other once the crews had been set for the Olympics.

For eight of the women training for the team, three scullers and five sweep oarswomen, 1988 is at least their second Olympics. They range in age from twenty-three to thirty-one. They have been teammates for a long time. Their relationships with one another are complicated, based on the dual premise of camaraderie and competition. They are the only ones who really know what each of them is going through in training so hard and shooting for the dream of the Olympics. They are competing for the same few seats in the crews. Any one athlete always wants the group to be equal in ability and competitive at the highest possible level — but with herself as a first among the equals. But paradoxically, she knows that if her best is still the lowest ranked in the crew, it's going to be an even faster crew.

Until the crews are set, the Seoul Olympic Games remain somewhat nebulous. They are the goal of all the training, but will remain only a name and a date until racing time comes in mid-September. "This Olympics is less focused to a particular event right now than the last two Olympics, when I knew I was in the pair," says Tricia Smith, the oldest woman on the team. "It's harder to imagine what's really going to be happening. But our training will be as focused later when we get the crew together."

At thirty-one, Tricia is the veteran. The rest of the team draws strength from her experience and confidence, and rows to the stable rhythm she sets in the boat. Tricia makes everything look easy. Her movements are deliberate, her manner understated. She has olive skin, brown eyes and rich chestnut hair that she combs back into a ponytail for rowing. When she is rowing, she always has to have her oar set at exactly the same angle because she is so sensitive to its feel. Once she has that, she can weather any storm that rages in the rest of the boat.

Tricia is a remarkable athlete in both her talent and her persistence. Although almost unknown in Canada, she was a bronze or silver medallist at World Championships or Olympic Games in eight out of the past ten years. In 1976 she participated in the first Olympic rowing events for women, and in the same year she watched her younger sister, Shannon Smith, win a bronze medal in swimming. Tricia's whole family is athletic — her mother was on the Pan American basketball team, and her father was an all-star rugby player. Although he was confined to a wheelchair after a back operation, he continues to play a wide range of sports and swims every day. At Whistler, near their Vancouver home, he still downhill skis in specially designed equipment. He raised the seed money with Rick Hansen for the Man-In-Motion worldwide tour.

Jane Tregunno, who stroked the four in 1987, is, like Tricia, a consistent top performer. At twenty-six, she is already rowing on her third Olympic team. Before starting rowing at sixteen, Jane had reached the national level in swimming. She was attracted to rowing partly because she grew up in a house overlooking the Henley course in St. Catharines, Ontario.

"When I started rowing, I hated carrying down the boat," recalls Jane. "It was so heavy and it killed my shoulders. I was six feet one inch and 125 pounds, while everyone else was way shorter. The best rowing would be when we got to the club and the boat was already on the dock, and then somebody needed it afterwards." Lithe, blonde Jane no longer bends like a reed under the boat. She has gained a good twenty-five pounds of muscle over the last ten years, and on the national team all the women are tall.

"In my first spring, I planned to be the average teenager, and have fun and work for the summer," says Jane. "And then I started rowing on the junior national team, and that changed everything. I thought, 'Hey, I could do this at a pretty serious level.' Although I didn't really realize what I was doing. I was having fun and we were going to get to travel. I remember seeing my swim coach right at the final testing for the team selection. He said, 'Well, what happens if you make the team?' I said we were going to Belgrade, Yugoslavia, and he said, 'What are you going to try next year, table tennis? I hear they're going to Japan.' He was hurt that I'd left swimming and thought I just wanted the trip."

Jane took to rowing like a duck to water, winning a bronze in the junior eight that summer and a junior gold in Moscow in 1979. Then she made the national team and earned an Olympic silver in 1984. She comes across as sweet and gracious, but under her polite exterior she knows exactly what she wants. "I love the power I get from rowing, the feeling you have when you are doing something you are really good at," she admits.

"Andrea Schreiner has been through the meat grinder," says Jim Joy, the director of Canadian rowing. Andrea is on her third Olympic team as well. At five feet ten inches and 155 pounds, Andrea is just about the average size among the Canadian national team women. She has blue eyes, baby-fine brown hair that she wears cropped short, and a sudden, wide smile. Like her teammates, she is strong-willed, forthright and passionate. She grew up in St. Catharines, where her parents owned a ski shop and where the sport of rowing reigns supreme. She made her first national team in 1977 at eighteen. As an athlete, Andrea has shown great consistency and also adaptability. Over the years she has finished in fourth place at the World Championships in every event, both sculling and sweep.

"In my good years, I've known what I wanted to do and how to do it. I haven't wavered," says Andrea. "When I've been more wishy-washy, things haven't gone so well." She came a disappointing eleventh in the double in 1987. That year, she had tried simultaneously to finish her master's in physiology at the University of Victoria, coach rowing, be on the executive of the Victoria Rowing Club and recover from the break-up of her marriage. To top it all off, persistent crew changes over the summer gave Andrea and her partner just three weeks to practise together.

"When you do something, do it properly, not half-assed," advises Andrea, coming out of 1987. She speaks emphatically, leaning forward. "That's how I've attacked rowing at my best — doing it so I can be the best I can be and better than anybody else out there."

"I like single sculling because I like having control over my own destiny," says Andrea, who dominated Canadian sculling between 1980 and 1984. "If things don't go well in the system, you can always go to train on your own and come back in later on. You can say, 'You're wrong, I am better than you think I am,' and then show them! For 1988 I've got some catching up to do. But there's only one thing to do, and that's to try. I'm going back to what's worked for me before." Andrea is putting herself on the line for Seoul by training in Italy. There she can row and work in a focused environment and reach her potential again.

For inspiration and confidence, Andrea looks to a race in 1980 when she felt she was particularly on track. That year, she was one of the top-ranked single scullers in the world. The Canadian boycott of the Moscow Olympics thwarted her hope for Olympic gold.

"The Lucerne Rotsee Regatta in June that year was, unofficially anyway, the Western world's Olympics. With the exception of the Romanians, everyone who went to the Olympics was there. Lucerne couldn't have gone better. I won the first day and came third the next. Both the races, especially the one that I won, are still vivid in my mind except for the portion where I blanked out. I sort of went into a trance where I was so focused that I can't remember it. And then all of a sudden I came out of it with about two hundred metres to go and I was in the lead. And I thought, 'Wow, I'm leading the race! Let's keep going!' It was a really neat experience.

"After Lucerne we went to a training camp in Meschede, West Germany. Jack, my coach, still has the video of how I was rowing at the camp. You can just see the focus in the way I was rowing. It was aggressive, it was ready. I was wired for sound and ready to spring. I was on the edge and staying on the correct side of the edge, not falling over it.

"Shortly after we got to Meschede, I got a call that my father was very sick. I went home and he died two weeks later. The Olympics started a week and a half after that, about July 20. In retrospect, I couldn't have raced at the Olympics even if they had happened, just because of what happened in my personal life. I went for a major downslide after that. People told me I changed. I sort of lost the killer instinct you have to have in the single. Between 1981 and 1984, I was there in body but not in mind. Each year was my attempt to get back to where I had been in 1980. But in 1984 I rowed really well. My Olympic final was one of my best races. I missed the bronze but only by inches — I just didn't have as much at the finish as the girl who came third. But it had been back and forth between us for the whole race. So that's how it's been in my career; there have been these hills and valleys."

Silken Laumann and Kay Worthington are Andrea's major competition in Canada. The Seoul Games will be their second Olympics. Silken, Kay and Andrea have all placed fourth in the single at World Championships, despite their different strengths. Only one of them will race the single at the 1988 Olympics. The other two will have to assess their chances in crew boats. They will then face other athletes vying for crew boats.

Silken Laumann's ups have been the rewards of her extraordinary natural ability; her downs, the result of repeated injuries. Silken's first year on the national team was in 1983. That spring she had rowed her novice season for her high school in Mississauga. From the start, she was fast, although she barely knew how to hold her sculls. In 1984 she teamed up with her older sister Daniele to win a bronze medal at the Olympics in the double sculls. Silken's body is a glorious athletic instrument. She trains passionately, but not always within the bounds of good sense. A teammate says of her, "She has a driving force in her that is superhuman." Silken has not yet had an injury-free World Championships. She still has to learn what pain is so that she heeds its warnings enough not to do permanent damage. At twenty-three, Silken is five feet eleven inches and 165 pounds, all of it lean, sinewy muscle. She is a youthful Valkyrie, a Nordic warrior goddess. She has five years yet before she reaches her prime and the sky is her limit.

Silken has white blonde hair and a smile that lights up her face like a 150-watt light bulb. One can picture her best in electric turquoises and vibrant pinks. A wild spirit, she fairly quivers with excitement, as if there were music coursing through her that only she can hear. Perhaps this explains the November night when she kicked off her shoes and danced alone through the rainy Victoria streets. She returned an hour and a half later with blistered feet.

Kay Worthington, who represented Canada in the single in 1987, is the only Canadian oarswoman to qualify directly for the Olympic Games in Seoul. At twenty-eight, Kay has been on the national team for six years. She rowed sweep from 1981 to 1984 and then switched to sculling. Like Andrea, she craved the control that being in a single gave her. She moved from her native Toronto to Philadelphia in 1985 to train.

Kay's teammates tease her about being "Kay for scuttlebutt," since she so avidly follows all the rowing gossip. But she devours newspapers with the same voracity, from the local daily to the *Economist*. When Kay lets down her classically bobbed brown hair, she is infectious fun. She has had to learn to control her ferocious intensity. In 1983 at the World Championships, Kay once woke up in the night, clutched the woman she was rooming with and cried, "I'm scared shitless!" The woman, who prided her own sangfroid about her rowing, didn't appreciate being disturbed. She decided Kay was a fanatic. Long-legged Kay is fast in a single because she is very determined, very fit and very sensitive to the way her boat moves through the water.

The athlete who wins the single trials has a pretty clear idea that she will row the single in the Olympics. But the picture blurs for the crew boats, especially in cases where athletes are possible contenders in both sculling and sweep. After 1984, like Kay, many sweep athletes learned to scull. The coaches encouraged the trend, modifying the team selection procedures to minimize the differences between sweep and sculling. Moving from sweep to sculling is like going from freestyle to the backstroke in swimming. The same basic motions apply, but the athlete has to work to modify her technique. Only when the stroke becomes second nature can the rower relax and concentrate on speed and power — and winning World Championship medals. The coaches hoped the top athletes would develop enough versatility to compete in whichever event seemed to give them the best chance of winning the gold. Unfortunately, some top athletes got caught in the switching back and forth.

Lisa Robertson has competed in both sweep and sculling, despite her desire to concentrate on sweep alone. Lisa is close to the magical six feet in height and carries the weight that rowers envy. However, she has had to work hard to prove herself. An only child, she grew up on a sailboat in the South Pacific. Her father is now a boat builder in Hawaii, and her mother lives by the sea on Vancouver Island. Lisa lives in her grandfather's old house in Victoria, surrounded by the maps and models that reflect his boat-building career. In 1983 she startled the members of her crew by saying, "Sometimes I wonder how I got here." Such self-doubt must have been put to rest when she won a bronze medal rowing starboard side in the coxed four in 1985.

Lisa has a relaxed attitude about life that she usually manages to transfer to rowing. Her way of dealing with the frustration of being put in a sculling boat for the 1986 World Championships was to look at the clouds for a while. Then things fell into place. She also finds her centre in the rowing itself. "I love doing it," she says simply. "The boat moving through the water is like art, it's an aesthetic motion. Rowing put me in touch with the physical part of myself and helped my development as a whole person. I really had to prove to myself I could do something like that."

For 1988, Lisa is committed to rowing sweep, where she feels she is strongest. Sick of being overlooked for the boat of her choice, she is training in the pair with Tina Clarke in Victoria. Since the winners of the pair trials can stay in that boat for the Olympics, Lisa and Tina want to ensure they have that option open if other possibilities fall through.

Twenty-eight-year-old Tina Clarke is a versatile athlete. Since her first World Championships in 1983, she has rowed both port and starboard, and in 1987 she even tried sculling. But for 1988 she wants to be where she can perform her best, which means staying in a sweep boat, training with one specific partner. Tina is a strategist. She sees clearly what she wants and then sets out to achieve her goal.

"I started rowing seriously because I wanted to be really successful in something, to feel like I was accomplishing something," explains Tina. "And rowing is a small enough thing that you can strive to perfect it, and in so doing become the best in the world. I especially love rowing in a crew because it is so rewarding to make a group of people work as one unit." Tina's almost artistic sensibility in rowing — her gift of blending with others — helped the coxed four win bronze medals in 1985 and 1986. Tina sat in three seat behind Tricia Smith, the stroke.

At five feet nine inches, both blonde Tina and her dark-haired older sister Heather are small for Olympic-class rowers. The sixth and seventh of nine children of a missionary in Africa, they grew up on a farm outside Woodstock, Ontario. They started rowing in high school. An article on Heather in a London, Ontario, newspaper in 1982 mortified her with its provocative heading, "Too pretty to row." "Heather has a certain nervous energy about her, an inner strength," it said. "She struggles just a little to keep an effervescent personality from bubbling over." Thirty-year-old Heather has been on the national team since 1979. The Clarke sisters have both fought for years to build up their weight and prove their talent as international competitors. They've kept on track by sheer strength of will. In 1988 Tina competes at a strong 155 pounds and Heather at 146 pounds. But that is still small.

The major competition in world rowing comes from the Eastern bloc countries. The Russians produce enough oarswomen at six feet two inches and 200 pounds that people think of all of them that way. The East Germans, Romanians and Bulgarians are right there with the Russians, getting their share of the medals, although they are more likely to be six feet tall and weigh 170 pounds. Several of the new athletes on the Canadian Olympic team are also this size. They will have their chance to prove their international calibre in Seoul if they make the Olympic standards in Lucerne in July 1988.

Canadian coaches not so secretly wish that *all* their oarswomen weighed 170 pounds. But, despite their smaller size, the Canadian women have won thirteen World Championship and Olympic medals since 1976.

"It's easy to look at it from the shore and put your finger on it," observed a Canadian coach, Ian McFarlane. "With the Russians, East Germans, Bulgarians, when you see them row and see their faces socially, there's an assurance there. You can get away with not being the physical equivalents of some of the Eastern bloc women if you are awfully, awfully aggressive, confident and sure of yourselves. And if you are a little better trained."

Olympic athletes build themselves up to their formidable heights of physical achievement by asserting their wills in training day by day over years. They have to put their living situation together in such a way that they have the space to achieve that kind of single-mindedness each day. Focusing themselves so much on one thing is risky because they have to put aside so many other things to do it. As Kay said about moving to Philadelphia, "Now that I've decided to move to the States and am rowing full time I have more on the line — it's like, 'Well, if I'm doing this full time, I'd better frigging well make sure I'm competitive. If I'm not competitive, what's the point?'" Such people are feisty. They won't give up until they want to, even when by all outside measures they should.

The rowers all hate rowing when the system dominates them. The rowing runaround is legendary and gets in the way of the physical part of the sport. Politics in the system, bad luck or disappointing performances can set people at odds and erode their confidence in themselves and each other. Then, because they've invested so much energy in it, rowing becomes a fish-hook. They can pull it out only with great pain.

Watching from the outside, the rest of the world doesn't know why athletes, and especially the women, stay in when things go bad. For men, doing a traditionally male sport like rowing is part of "becoming a man" and is therefore approved by society, at least for a few years. The women, by contrast, encounter the attitude that they might be better off doing something other than a strength sport. But other people can't know why athletes of either sex stay in, unless they too have wanted something so much they'd pay that kind of price for it. A medallist from 1984, Angie Schneider, found that she couldn't convey the rewards of rowing to her partner. She tried her best to explain it all to him but finally said, "You can't know."

"Nothing means that much to me," he responded. "Nothing. I'd never hurt like that for anything. I like life. Why should I hurt myself?"

The woman told her crewmates later, "He thinks we're a bunch of sickos."

Even some coaches wonder about their athletes' motives. Kathryn Barr, a cheerful and talented athlete and first-time Olympian in 1988, couldn't figure out why one of the national coaches kept delving into her reasons for rowing on the national team. "Can't he just accept that I don't have any dark needs to overcompensate for anything in my life? That I row because I like doing it?"

She has a point. The women on the team got into rowing and continue to row, when all is said and done, because rowing is about ecstasy. Who wouldn't want that? The physical ecstasy of being in top shape and celebrating the body's ability. The mental thrill of being so disciplined. Rowing is sometimes even about mystical ecstasy — of transcending the pain, rowing through it. Rowers love rowing because it gives their lives an intensity that compares to nothing else.

2

THE ZEALOTS

In his launch on a drizzly morning in early spring, the women's rowing coach, Drew Harrison, looks like a prime candidate for a "Man and the Sea" portrait. A black, floppy rain hat covers his thick sandy hair, and his athletic frame is insulated by a yellow rubberized rain suit — the high-tech version of the fisherman's cable-knit sweater. He is a rawboned six feet five inches. But at forty, Drew still has a somewhat boyish look, and he is pleased when people mistake him for an oarsman on the team. He sports a reddish mustache, and there is a pronounced cleft in his strong chin. His eyes are blue, with curly, blond-tipped lashes. The athletes like to imitate the slow blink of Drew's eyes. They also imitate his Philadelphian accent. Drew has a careful way of speaking and uses rowing jargon, like "huge [pronounced yuge], massive drive" and "the dynamicness of the legs."

"Coaching mature athletes is really neat," says Drew when asked about working with the older oarswomen on the 1988 team. "You may not be as much of a central figure if you coach someone who's really good as you would if you coach a novice program. Working with mature athletes is certainly not as immediately uplifting. Yet the challenges of helping good people get a slight bit better are really great. They work really really hard for just tiny increments of improvement. They are getting near the limits of mankind's ability as we currently understand it. That's an extraordinarily worthwhile personal challenge."

Drew followed the call of the oar from New York State to British Columbia. Hooked on rowing as a freshman at Syracuse University in 1964, he coached the men's freshman program there from 1972 to 1981. In 1981 he began coaching the women's varsity team at the University of British Columbia in Vancouver. In 1984 he coached the well-established competitors Tricia Smith and her partner, Betty Craig, in the Canadian national team pair. At the Los Angeles Olympics they won a silver medal. Since 1985, Drew has coached the Canadian women's coxed four, which has won two bronze medals at the World Championships.

"I like to have input from people and I like to develop a situation where the athlete has a major part in the decision, but at the same time, I want things to go the way I want them to go," Drew says. He is known for frequently asking the athletes how they feel during workouts. "Although sometimes I wonder if this image of having the athletes being involved in the decision-making process is just an illusion."

Athletes always need an outside assessment of their efforts in order to know what they should do to improve. Coaches are responsible for helping athletes realize their potential. Athletes' needs differ, depending on their personality, experience and confidence. Different athletes will perform better either with more room for autonomy or with more assistance at different times in their careers. Coaches and athletes do not always agree on how much the coach should step in to help, but the coach generally has the last word because he selects the crew. On the national team, however, a selection committee from Rowing Canada makes the final ruling.

"I still push people to work hard," Drew says. "Sometimes I push gently, sometimes not so gently. Sometimes I ask people to do things that are extraordinary, like give up months of a job, take off time from school."

Like Drew himself, the oarswomen emphasize the positive aspects of his coaching and of their relationship. Personal feelings they have about his approach depend partly on their previous experience with other coaches. Some of the women may object to the iron hand within Drew's velvet glove. Others would prefer Drew to be more authoritarian. As one athlete says, "With years of competition under our belts, we know ourselves and what we want from a coach pretty well. The professional relationship comes first." The athletes put aside their differences with Drew in order to work with him in the top crew.

Depending on the needs of the coach and the athlete, their relationship will be more or less personal. As long as it works well, it does not really matter what the dynamic is. Andrea Schreiner, for instance, has a fairly close relationship with one of the coaches she had in the single sculls over the past decade. She speaks of him as "a father figure."

"We spent a lot of time together and I really respected him. Jack is always up-front and down-to-earth. I learned to trust that. For training, he gave me what I needed to know in black and white. It's the execution of the race that's important. He would say, 'Here are the facts. You have to do this and this and the choice is yours. You're only going to do in the race what you've learned in practice.' And I need that. Racing scared me at first, but I learned that if I've done my homework and prepared my best, I won't choke. If I'm not going fast, tell me. Don't set me up for a failure down the road."

All athletes must be confident that they will perform when they go into competition or else risk making fools of themselves. That confidence comes from one factor alone — solid preparation in training. But everyone hopes that in racing they will hit the peak where rowing becomes poetry in motion. That kind of performance depends on the magic of being perfectly tuned to the moment. It depends on being psyched, and being at one with the crew and the boat. The coach can do a lot to inspire the athlete.

Problems arise, as they do in any close relationship, when each partner's assumptions about the other's needs and abilities are unrealistic. The coach must be attuned to the athlete's needs in order to help draw out the best performance. "When athletes haven't developed the kind of certainty in themselves that they need to have to win, it needs to be placed in them," observed a national team coach. "A gifted coach can do that. And athletes who are slightly unsure want the 'what the hell, take a shot at it' approach. I don't think that produces top-notch athletes in the long run, but it often gets results in the short term."

Coaches who take on too much of the responsibility to motivate the athlete can hurt the athlete's personal development. Such power relationships, hinging on the dominance of the coach over the submissive athlete, happen too often, particularly with young athletes.

"Young athletes, especially, want a guide," says Silken. "Coaches want to fall into that role because it is gratifying. Yet expecting the coach to alleviate all the pressure sets both of them up for disillusionment. One problem is that the oarswomen look for someone to give the easy answer, and when that answer doesn't come, we're disappointed. I spent a lot of time seeking a guide in my coaches. I've just realized that my performance and state of mind were my own responsibility. Now I can appreciate coaches in their role as technical helper and sounding board. Yet it's scary to discover that there's nothing special that will make you go faster, but you can't be motivated by someone else in the long run." However, even when an athlete matures, the pattern of dominance and submission may persist. Many coaches depend on that element of control and are reluctant to see themselves as "helper and sounding board."

Demystifying racing and the coach is often the athlete's first step to maturity. But seeing the coach as the central figure in one's life — as God — is a stage many developing athletes go through. Certain women athletes on the 1988 team were naive about sport when they started rowing. Many of them from traditional families and with traditional feminine attitudes, they were oriented towards pleasing authority figures, seeking approval and getting positive reinforcement.

Doug Clark and Rudy Wieler are two coaches who gave many of the older women on the team their start in national rowing as teenagers and young adults. Both of them larger-than-life characters, they had the energy and strength of will to create women's programs in the late 1970s, when Canadian women's rowing was in its fledgling stage. They both demanded intense commitment from the women they coached, to themselves as well as to their programs. The intensity of experience during their Doug years and their Rudy years formed the women's attitudes towards later coaches.

"Flat out 'til you pass out," said Doug Clark again. "You have to push to be a champion. Remember, you're competing with yourself. Go flat out 'til you pass out." On a blustery January day in 1977, eleven teenage girls from Woodstock Collegiate in Woodstock, Ontario, jerked their forty-pound barbells over their heads and then swung them down to their ankles to begin the exercise over again. Squat, stretch, squat, stretch. Sweat flew off their skinny arms and legs. Heather Clarke weighed 118 pounds, the crew average. Tina Clarke was the heaviest member at 130 pounds. Doug had to promote the virtues of persistence for them to be good. "Okay, stop now!" called Doug. "Check your pulse rates." The girls dropped their weights on the floor and bent over them. The only sound in the room was panting.

"At Woodstock we did all those weight circuits, as quickly as we could as hard as we could," recalls Heather. "We never knew how many minutes we would have to go. One time, I was so exhausted doing the circuit I was falling all over the mat, because I couldn't control my body. I couldn't imagine what it would be like to hurt any more than I already did. But I was also afraid we were going to stop before I had managed to pass out. Suddenly the lights went out. I crumpled on the sweaty, crackling mat. 'Did I pass out?' I quavered. The lights flickered on a moment later — there had been an electrical storm. I never lived that one down!

"To pass out, to die, to gain Doug's approval — that would have equalled the opening of heaven's gates to glory."

The physical release of athletic performance transported these kids into a different time and space. Average people though they were, they stretched themselves, pushing each other in training. They achieved a greatness that only they could appreciate, because only they knew the effort that went into it.

"If you have a goal, I'm going to continually move that goal away from you and push you a little harder," says Doug Clark. Doug is a visionary, his passion is development. "I don't look for size and weight for a good rower. I'm looking for far more personal things. I'm looking for determination, drive, focus."

Doug has recently terminated his contract as a national sculling coach and director of the High Performance Sport Centre in London, Ontario. At fifty, he is still fit, intense and charismatic, with his dark hair, hazel eyes and air of breeding. He is the only child of a professional football player and was himself recruited at the age of eighteen to play for the Winnipeg Blue Bombers. In fact, he started rowing to get in shape for football. He rowed competitively for fourteen years and won a silver medal in the double at the 1967 Pan American Games. When he retired from rowing, he became a stockbroker in Toronto. Rowing remained his passion, though, so he started the rowing program at Upper Canada College, a private boys' school in Toronto. Then in 1975, a wealthy businessman enticed him to Woodstock, offering to finance him as Canada's first professional rowing coach. Doug moved to Boston in 1980, first to coach at the Massachusetts Institute of Technology and then to start up a club program. He returned to Canada as a national team sculling coach in 1986.

"I think pride in what you can do is very important," Doug continues, "and pride in the program that you're a part of. I call that pride 'quiet arrogance.' That term obviously needs defining. It's so meaningful, you don't have to be vocal. You prove it on the water. You've got to be arrogant." Doug gave his heart to his athletes and expected their devotion in return. For some of the kids he coached, his attention turned their lives around. He gave them the confidence to dream. He had the energy to transform many of them into world-class athletes at the junior and Olympic level.

Stephen Beatty was one of four cigarette-smoking boys at Woodstock Collegiate Doug persuaded to row. His life changed because of rowing. He decided not to drop out of high school. He went to an Ivy League university and became captain of the rowing team there. He rowed in the 1984 Olympics. Stephen says, "Doug kept us in a cocoon, inside which we competed beyond ourselves to achieve excellence. The rest of the world was mediocre. Doug Clark was a zealot — I became a zealot. Even now, for me, things have to be perfect. I have a mental need for it."

Doug set the tone for the larger-than-life rowing experiences yet to come by taking his novices from Woodstock Collegiate down to Philadelphia for a training camp in 1976. He solemnly warned them of racial troubles and gang warfare in the area near their hotel. Heather, for one, felt completely overwhelmed. With her excitable nature she was already set, in this overcharged atmosphere, to believe Doug completely when he drew her aside into his blue van.

"Heather, if you want to, you can go to the Olympics!" Doug said. Heather took these precious words and pondered them in her heart. She was the anointed one, and she didn't dare tell sisters and teammates for fear they would be consumed with jealousy. Never mind the fact that she started crying from fright the first time she got into a boat. And never mind the fact that she soon learned that the Olympic dream had been imparted to others.

These people were naive to believe him. However, Doug proved he could develop young people. He knew how to coach rowers up to world-class standard. In 1977 the Woodstock crew were Canadian champions. In 1978 Tina Clarke and Christine Cybulski won bronze medals at the Junior World Championships. In 1979 Heather made the national team and Christine stroked the Canadian junior eight to a gold medal at the World Championships at Moscow. Three of Doug's Woodstock athletes were on the 1984 Olympic team.

"Rowing is a vehicle," Doug says. "You develop a strong person and then you develop a strong oarsperson and it's often in that order. I get excited about someone who absolutely refuses to lose. Now there's a different definition of competing." But Doug focuses so much on the ideal of perpetual development and rowing as an allegory of life that it seems to the athletes he loses sight of racing.

Tina Clarke took exception to Doug's attitude early on. The sixth daughter in a warm and high-spirited evangelical family, Tina already knew what her values were. "I just wanted Doug to show me how to get from A to B in a boat the fastest I could."

Doug told Tina that she would never go anywhere in rowing, that she did not have what it takes. Tina did not believe him.

"For Doug there were the 'chosen' — the ones who would be Olympians, and the ones who would not," recalls Tina. "Doug wanted to be central to the development of those chosen ones. I wasn't interested in blindly following a coach, even then. Because I wasn't devoted to him and thus, in his opinion, demonstrating my devotion to rowing, Doug didn't trust me to train. He told me to phone him every night to report what I had done that day. I said, 'I'm not going to phone you. You can believe me. I'm training hard.'" Rather than be intense all the time, she preferred to show the world her fun-loving side. Heather remembers listening to the thumps of Tina upstairs in her bedroom, doggedly doing her 500 nightly jump-squats holding a ten-pound weight. Then the phone would ring, and it would be Doug wanting to know why Tina had not called yet. Had she skipped training?

"The best one of all was him phoning me about my attitude," remembers Tina. "He told me he didn't like me or the kind of person I was, and how I'd never go anywhere. I got fed up and hung up on him."

Tina got out of Woodstock the following summer by going to St. Catharines and rowing on the junior national team for Rudy Wieler. In a way, she jumped out of the frying pan of one coach who demanded control, into the fire of another. Doug and Rudy sometimes used methods that shocked their athletes' parents, but both coaches accomplished what they set out to do. They created disciplined world-class competitors out of motley teenagers. Today those former teenagers appreciate the lessons learned, even though they wonder at the cost. "Doug would say, 'I leave it up to you to train, that's your decision,' and Rudy would scream and make sure we held him in fear. The two of them were really doing the same thing, making us put out. Yet Doug was preoccupied with having us train. He taught us how to do race-length pieces till our legs fell off, and keep doing them, but he never had us put it altogether on the line for just one. Rudy, on the other hand, thought, 'We're going to teach these girls how to race.' Doug taught us how to row, and Rudy taught us how to go balls out. That summer in youth, I learned how to race."

Born in 1944 to a Mennonite family in Saskatchewan, Rudy Wieler grew up in St. Catharines. Heavyset and short, he never excelled in sports, although he was always a keen participant. In 1960, when he was sixteen, he watched the Rome Olympics on television. He decided that he wanted to go to the Olympics himself, but he knew it would be as a coach rather than as an athlete. A high school geography teacher in St. Catharines, he coached high school and youth men's rowing for several years, as well as volleyball and football. Every team he coached he brought to championship quality.

"If you win," says Rudy, "and someone asks you how you did, you only have to say two words. I won. If you finish in any other place, from silver to last, you have to make excuses. I don't want to have to make any excuses." Though asked to be the junior national volleyball coach, he chose to go with rowing instead. In 1977 he was asked to set up the women's youth program, and he accepted: "I saw the opportunity, and I said, 'Good, let's go for it.'" From 1981 to 1986 he was the national team coach, and in that role he affected many of the women who are going for the 1988 team. In 1984 he realized his dream of going to the Olympics and watched his coxed four win a silver medal. At present he is taking a breather from coaching, but he plans to return.

"You cannot get kids in our society to play anymore unless there is the possibility to win," says Rudy. "Therefore, you try to bring kids along to play the game very quickly, at whatever expense and cost, okay? When I coached youth one of the things that people accused me of was burning kids out too early. Well, I say hogwash to that. That wasn't me, that was a societal thing. And besides, we all benefited. Many of the kids were students of mine in school who would have ended up never being first in anything and they ended up being champions. A lot of teachers came to me and said, 'Can you get this kid into rowing? It will straighten him out.' Most of the young athletes I've coached have ended up coming back to me in later years and saying, 'Geez, now I've finally figured out what it was all about.' And it fits. But the price I had to pay, to set myself up as the overall orchestrator of things, was a high one. I don't appreciate the image that I was painted."

Rudy enjoyed running his own ship. Yet despite his get-tough approach, he felt he bonded strongly to his girls. In 1980, when much of the youth eight got sick at the World Championships, Rudy himself hurt his foot: "I look back now and feel I got sick too in sympathy with my crew. If it hadn't been the races at the World Championships, I wouldn't have had those girls row." The crew didn't see it that way. They saw him get angry more often. During practice he rode a bicycle along the shore and coached from there. One day as they were rowing along, they heard a big crash and a howl from Rudy, followed by curses. He must have tripped over a root or something and fallen off his bicycle. They had to row away very fast so he would not hear them laughing about his ingrown toenail.

"I started thinking about trying out for the 1980 Olympic team in the fall of 1979," says Jane Tregunno, who rowed for

Rudy on the youth team. "I remember talking about it lying down in the back of a station wagon on the way to a regatta in Connecticut. Finally I got the courage to tell Rudy. He was very good about arranging schools for me, and everything, but he immediately took me out of the eight. I was condemned to rowing in the pair with him a couple of times. In the boat I could pull him around because he's so short and I had so much leverage with my height. When everyone else rowed by in the eight I sort of looked over and moaned."

Rudy moved up to coaching the national team the second year Jane was on it, in 1981.

"In youth, Rudy did all our thinking for us, directed everything," remembers Jane. "On the senior team, people did what they wanted. It was good for me to come from Rudy, because I learned to be competitive and disciplined — everyone worked like crazy all the time — but Rudy had to learn he couldn't control everyone."

"I had difficulty dealing with these people as young adults, not high school students," admits Rudy. "I definitely came to better grips with that as I moved on." Although his behaviour towards them sometimes wore them down, the women could sometimes laugh about it. One day during Rudy's first summer, he pulled the women's eight together after practice. It had been pouring rain, and they had left their extra shirts in the boat bay to keep them dry. As soon as they put away their boat, they dashed over to get their shirts. But Rudy called them back to help carry up the motorboat. Everyone hated doing that because it was so awkward and heavy. The women felt a little self-conscious in their clinging wet T-shirts. Wouldn't you know that some of them had worn white! Bras were a useless article of clothing as far as many of them were concerned — they didn't fit anyway, with chests that measured thirty-nine inches and most of that girth in the latissimus dorsi muscles in the back. After the coach boat was put away, Rudy summoned up his courage. In his most respectful voice, which still carried the authority of a high school teacher, he said, "I want you girls to wear bras from now on to the practice. There are a lot of high school boys around here, and I want you young ladies to set a good example of modesty." Or at least, that's the way the women remember it. They also remember that it only worked for about two days.

Even though the national team oarswomen were more independent of Rudy than the youth girls had been, they still orbited around him. In 1981 there were two coxswains on the team. One was Lesley Thompson, who is on the 1988 team. She was new to Rudy Wieler, although she had rowed with some of the women at Western and she'd been on the 1980 Olympic team. In June, Rudy, after giving his own opinion, asked the crew going to the Royal Henley Regatta in England which coxswain they preferred. His bottom line was that Lesley was overweight. She weighed 104 pounds instead of the required 99. Very much attuned to what Rudy wanted, the crew chose the other coxswain, whom Rudy knew because she had been in his youth eight for two years. Lesley was devastated by the perfidy of her friends. Before leaving for England, the athletes had to endure a cold war. Lesley was going to prove that she could be down to weight before they left. She was. Moreover, her weight was never an issue again.

The coxswain can, on occasion, find herself torn in her commitment to both the crew and the coach.

"Our first morning back from the Henley we were exhausted and jet-lagged, but nonetheless did a twenty-four-kilometre workout," remembers Heather. "I had been leaning away from my rigger, which is a technical fault, that whole spring and early summer of 1981. I had been particularly frustrated by it when we were at the Henley, but Rudy strongly denied there was a problem. I was not going to be able to change it overnight, so I guess he wanted to minimize my pre-race anxiety. But I just got more worried.

"When we got home to Canada, Rudy put me in stroke seat of the eight, where I faced the coxswain. During that first practice, I leaned out of the boat. About halfway through, Rudy zoomed up to the stern of the shell and pulled a wooden paddle out of his coach boat. 'Heather Clarke,' he said, 'if you're going to row like an animal, then we're going to have to treat you like an animal.' He gave the coxswain a paddle to hit me with every time I leaned out of the boat. Even now it's hard to laugh at the absurdity of the situation. The coxswain laid the paddle on the gunwhale of the shell so that I would feel it at the finish of the stroke. Then she pleaded with me not to lean out of the boat."

The coxswain acts as a liaison between crew and the coach. She can make an immense impact on her crew through her sensitivity to the feel of the boat, her reading of the members of the crew and how to motivate them, and her quick assessment of the competition and the moves they will make. She is not the one who sets the rhythm of the crew, and contrary to popular opinion, she does not yell, "Stroke! Stroke!" And rowers hate it when non-initiates call out "Stroke" from the shore. The person rowing in stroke seat sets the cadence, and the rowers behind her watch and follow her. Lesley Thompson, the 1988 Olympic team coxswain, is fastidious; she has the mix of perfectionism and ruthlessness that makes the athletes really glad she's on their team and not someone else's.

Living by the unforgiving rule that only winning was good enough, Rudy was very demanding of his athletes. He says that he's come a long way since those days. "In my early days of coaching, I was a very caustic, negative person. And the feedback people got did not generate good feelings. I guess I thought they probably feared me a little bit. Only I always used the word 'respect.' People thought — 'I'll do it to spite the son-of-a-gun.' I missed the boat there. I was lucky I got what I got. Hey, we always talk about praising little kids — well, you know what? I react pretty well to praise too, and I'm a big kid. But we forget that. I make a point in my life now of trying to go out and tell people to have a good day, and if they do something I thought they deserved praise for, I let them know."

People forgave Rudy for his temper as long as he got results. At the Junior World Championships in Yugoslavia in 1978, he played the heavy to keep the fifteen- to eighteen-year-olds on track. "In the speeches I gave," explains Rudy, "I had to wean the girls away from me, because they had to race it themselves."

"We were finally having some rest after being beaten into the ground all summer by work," recalls Jane, "and I'm sure we were going a little crazy. The night before our race Rudy gave us that famous pep talk about 'You girls are the biggest bunch of disjointed bitches I ever met, and if you get your heads screwed on straight you may come in sixth.' We were annoyed and thought — 'We'll show him.' It worked." They won a bronze medal. And the next year, the eight won a gold medal in Moscow. Rudy became a power in the land. His youth girls saw him as omniscient, omnipotent. To be one of "Rudy's girls" was the pinnacle of success.

Unfortunately, at the senior level the medals were more elusive. In 1982 the Canadian women's eight came a disappointing fifth in their final at the World Championships. In the fall-out, Rudy sent the crew a letter indicating his disappointment. In the preliminary heat, the women had lost to the Americans by only some hundredths of a second. Yet the Americans had gone on to win a silver in the final. "Those athletes in the 1982 eight, I told them they should soul search," Rudy says. The women in the crew felt that by writing the letter Rudy was removing himself from responsibility for the final race. They were furious. Rudy said he wanted the women to share the responsibility for the fifth place showing because he had to answer to people for it.

"The letter made us feel that Rudy didn't trust the athletes," says Kay Worthington. "We had looked to him for the answers and this made us feel that he didn't have them, and maybe our ideas were valid. What did that mean about training programs and how he qualified us to be there? There was an extreme sense of disappointment and injustice." Kay led the women in a protest against Rudy.

Although Jane did not see the situation in as black-and-white terms as Kay, she was concerned about the coaching. She had taken the summer of 1982 off. "I felt a conflict because Rudy had done a lot for me, but I agreed with what was going on. I thought we did need a change. At that point, I didn't know if Rudy was the one to take us one step further. He phoned me and asked me if I could help him. He said how he'd made concessions for me in 1979 when I hurt my knee. I said, 'I am trying to help you. Maybe you'll learn from this. I can't betray my friends.' Also, it made me angry because I had earned my way, even though he had been good to me. He had to change."

Rowing Canada suggested that Rudy hire an assistant. "I soul searched, and I changed, and I grew," says Rudy. "It was exciting, but very traumatic. Probably more significant for me than even the athletes realize. I was a thirty-eight-year-old man, and yet those people who were younger and more able to change, some of them haven't. They missed the boat. We could all have grown together. After 1982, I changed. Up to 1982, I included all. I had been caustic and maybe callous, but I included all. After that I became more introspective and sensitive in a way, but in another way I was more selfish. I concentrated on my own crew. I watched very carefully from 1982 on, and my focus was only on those athletes who were prepared to come with me." Rudy made the coxed four the priority crew for 1983 and 1984, and another coach took on the eight.

"In our 1984 four, things went really well," recalls Barb Armbrust. Barb grew up in St. Catharines and rowed under Rudy on the youth team in 1980. Because of her incredible strength, she made the coxed four in both 1983 and 1984. She also rowed in the four in 1985 when the crew won the bronze. She is a strong contender on the 1988 team. "In 1984 Rudy lost a lot of weight, changed his perspective on things, felt more confident. He became more sedate, open to comments. We felt that he was as much into the crew goal as we were."

"In 1983, though," recalls Kay, "Rudy was still directing us. We rowed in St. Catharines with the four. In 1984 we were at a different site from Rudy and his four. Not having a strong figure there even to rebel against made the whole thing disintegrate at the Olympics." The eight lost even a negative crew focus when they lost Rudy. They had their own coach, but crew morale dropped over the summer as the frustration at not getting it together mounted. The eight came fourth at Los Angeles in a miserable race.

Rudy was very much aware of the negative but powerful elements in his relationship with the eight. "Maybe I should have motivated them at the Olympics, but I felt that if I had got involved, they would have done it to spite me, not because of me. And I thought, 'That goes against everything I've now reconciled myself not to do. I want to work with positives.' And I said, 'No thanks. You ladies have got to do it on your own, and I'll take care of myself and my people.' Right or wrong, that was my decision. I don't know if those girls see it that way. But I felt so bad for them. When those young ladies had their opportunity to do what they could do, they didn't do it."

Going from naive trust in the coach's ability to mature confidence in themselves and the coach is a rocky road for many athletes. Some quit before they get there, either out of frustration with the system or because they fall behind as athletes. The ones who stay learn to play the game. Heather comments: "I went through several different stages. Under Doug, I had a naive belief in the rowing ethos. As an intense twenty-two-year-old I became disillusioned with Rudy. Now, at the grand old age of thirty, with Drew I find that my belief is tempered. My trust now has to be earned. The thing is, it's difficult not to associate your own changes in attitude with the coaches you had when you went through them, because being with them reminds you of things you may not like to remember."

Coaches, as well as athletes, suffer from reminders of their pasts. In 1986 Tina and Tricia won the pair trials. They could have been the national team pair, but they chose to try out for the coxed four. Lisa was designated to the pair after trying out unsuccessfully for the four. She thought that since she was in the pair she could choose her own coach. She didn't realize that only the pair who had won the trials had that option. When she chose

Drew, Rudy was angry. He had been appointed the women's pair coach.

"Athletes want nothing more than on a yearly basis to have the coach discard what happened the year before and treat them as fresh new beings," Rudy complained. "'I'm different this year, coach. Now select me! Be fair with me! Throw all those things away!' And we coaches, we're miracle men. We have to take all that stuff, information, and put it aside and treat you new. Boy, I wish they would do the same thing for a coach."

The system depends on both coaches and athletes maintaining trust in each other, although the coaches hold the balance of power because they choose the crews. When that trust is not there, both sides get hurt.

"I know that I'm difficult sometimes," admits Drew. "That isn't always a smart thing to do. If you get difficult, people will recognize it and there will be less interest in putting up with the guy. And if you see certain athletes as unmanageable, you'll look at them and think of problems instead of thinking of speed. Yet if a person has ability, it's a matter of how to help them develop it. And if part of the so-called difficulty in a person is something that can be developed into a strength instead of a difficulty, then not only do you eliminate the difficulty, but you make the crew go faster. That's desirable. But if the combination of abilities of coach and athlete is such that you cannot turn the difficulty into a strength, then it becomes a liability."

"But those are the people you want on the team," fires back one oarswoman. "Those are the elite athletes, people who have their own minds. You don't want to race with people who say, 'Oh yes sir, no sir.' You've got to have people who are tough, and you're not tough if you just say, 'Yes coach.'"

3

WINNING AND LOSING

When the athletes imagine what the 1988 Olympic Games in Seoul will be like, most of their reveries are confined to their own event. The dream of perfect execution after years of honing their highly specialized skills. At night, their leaden bodies sink as dead weights into their beds, but their minds wander effortlessly. They dream of stooping forward to receive the medal around their neck, and then they picture straightening, raising up their arms in victory. Tingles go down their spines, their hearts race. Then, as they are drifting off to sleep, their beds become the boat, gently rocking in the lap, lap, of the waves.

Seoul is a race, a date, a place. Nothing more. The political realities threaten to intrude, but even they seem remote, other worldly. None of the rowers at Seoul were in Munich in 1972, and their recollections of the murdered Israeli athletes are vague. Several remember the 1980 boycott. Many remember the 1984 boycott, but because they got to participate, it seems less significant. Instead they remember the Hollywood glitz of Los Angeles, since it was the first time of actually competing at the Olympics for all of these women except Tricia. As a result, Los Angeles is the Olympic measuring stick most have for Seoul. In L.A. no one had worries about what was happening in the rest of the world. In fact, for them the usual set of rules that govern the world had stopped. The focus was on sport. The buzz was in the air of Los Angeles itself — the athletes felt it when they arrived. The buzz was a real high, a confidence booster.

The environment in Seoul will have the surreal elements of any Olympic Games. But it will be different from Los Angeles. While the facilities themselves in Seoul are newly built and highly praised, athletes will have to orient themselves to the sight of Third World inequities. The Korean government wants to highlight its economic success, and in preparation for the Olympics the slums of Seoul are being razed. But the many homeless may make their presence felt.

These rowers have never raced in a Third World country before, as during the 1980s the World Championships were all in Europe. Thus, aside from the possibly unstable political situation, they will suffer culture shock from more elementary things like different food, beds, the hot climate. In Los Angeles, food of every possible national cuisine was provided for the athletes. Presumably much the same effort will be put forward in Seoul to ensure the athletes' comfort, but they must be prepared to adapt to differences. In Seoul the rowers will stay in the main Olympic village with athletes from other sports, since the human-made rowing course is in the 750-acre Olympic park.

When they arrived at the opening ceremonies in L.A., the athletes soon realized that the Olympic Games are an enormous enterprize. It was a swelteringly hot day. They drove in buses through crowded slums under police surveillance, and then were cloistered in an arena for hours while the festivities went on. The TV screen showing the festivities they were missing wasn't working. They were sticky and tired and bored. After aeons they were called to walk over to the stadium. They slowly wound their way through the crowded streets, eating the orange slices they'd been given to keep from becoming dehydrated. Security held the masses back, the masses who wanted to touch, see, belong. Finally the Canadians joined the pool of other athletes waiting their turn to enter the celebration. Brazilian athletes in their soft yellow and pale blue, Guatemalan athletes in their woven sombreros and embroidered reds. The Canadians in their red rugby-style specials from Sears.

"The most exciting thing at the 1984 Olympics for me," recalls Tina, "was going down the chute into the Olympic stadium. We were one of the first countries, 'C,' and we were a big country in terms of the number of athletes competing. All of a sudden, other performers for the opening ceremonies were around us, clapping their hands as we went down the chute. We all started running and screaming and cheering for ourselves. The stadium was just a flood of red. It was such a rush to go — 'We're here!' — and then come into the stadium. Everyone was on their feet, cheering for us. I thought, 'I can't believe this!' For us as rowers it was so unexpected. We were warned about this beforehand because we have so little contact with the media — people being in awe of us because we are Olympians just doesn't happen in rowing. The adoration experience is really unusual. We thought, 'Oh, it's no big deal, we can handle it.' But it was amazing."

In 1984 the rowers were cloistered away in Santa Barbara with only each other and the paddlers there. They had less opportunity to be overwhelmed by the enormity of the Games. The rowers on the different national teams knew each other quite well from years of World Championship racing anyway, so being with each other did not increase the pressure beyond what would normally be expected. They competed between 7 and 10 a.m., for after mid-morning the desert heat and winds made Lake Casitas unrowable. Since rowers always practise early in the morning, they were happy to stick to their usual schedule. Many events in Seoul are being scheduled in the morning as well, but this time to satisfy North American prime-time viewers, twelve hours away.

Even though the Olympic environment is set up so that the athletes can focus solely on their sport, there are enough distractions to upset anyone. It is an act of will by each athlete to stay on target. In 1984 Angie Schneider, one of the women in the coxed four, said her crew had to talk out what focus meant. "Jane and I roomed together, and Marilyn and Barb roomed together. One day Jane and I walked back into our room, and a magazine article with underlinings and circles was there, called 'Olympic Glory and the Also-Rans.' Jane and I at first were indignant that someone was trying to tell us we were 'also-rans.' They got involved in the social side — and we were having fun.

"The also-ran article was by a former Olympic athlete, who said he could sit and watch and say, 'That person's going to medal and that person's just here for the experience, the ride.' And we thought, 'Did Rudy put this here?' And then we found out that he had given it to a fellow crewmate, Barb, to read and pass on to us. Barb had fun too, but was more focus-focus than we were. We asked Barb if she thought we were also-rans. She said no, but that she could see this distinction in other crews. And I agreed, after talking to Barb. But it's difficult. The also-ran — who may be more balanced mentally, but that's not the point — the also-ran allows in other things, like the parades and the opening ceremonies. It became part of our race-preparation dialogue, this term and this distinction-drawing."

In 1984 the coxed four did things in practice that the coach felt would prepare them for the toughest battle of their lives. Angie describes what coach and crew meant by focus — they weren't talking about mental balance. "One day at the end of an exhausting practice we did a 1,000-metre piece with Rudy calling it, not Lesley. There we were, going through the same motion, over and over again, like the tic-toc in front of your eyes. And he was saying in a monotone voice, '*Now* you're feeling this, and *now* the pain will feel so bad you can't bear it, but you'll walk through. And you're going to be tough.' Brainwashing. I don't know if Rudy did it intentionally, but we saw it. At the end we were crying. Barb was crying because she was in pain, and Jane and I were crying because of what he was doing." Total focus makes people push beyond themselves. It's a big question — how to push yourself to the limit, how to extend your limit gradually over years of practice, so that when the moment comes you're ready to spring, and yet keep on the inside edge of destruction.

Barb recalls pulling up to the Olympic rowing course for the first time: "The grandstand was all the Olympic colours — the greens and pinks and golds — very soft and modern. Then we saw the finish line and smiled at each other. We knew exactly what the others in the crew were thinking about. It was just like — what a feeling, that moment." The familiar and reassuring moment of crossing the line — the moment that matters most to the rowers.

On the first weekend in August 1984, Heather perched at the finish line of the 2,000-metre rowing course at Lake Casitas. She watched her teammates race, her sister race, her boyfriend race. With the other spectators she watched the start of the races over the TV monitor, and then strained to see the crews pull the last 500 metres to the finish line. The TV monitors showed the close-up picture, the strain, the rhythm in the boat. When she watched the course, Heather could see all six boats jockeying together, could see the excitement, the speed of the approach. The lane markers over the finish line waved gently, detached from the frenzy of the crowd as the boats raced to the end. The noise would climb in crescendo. Then the horn would go off to mark the winner, and the tension would diminish into a buzz of cheering and discussion.

As team alternate, Heather did not race. Instead, that memorable weekend, she watched her peers collect their medals. On Saturday the Romanians, the only Eastern bloc athletes who did not boycott the Olympics, made almost a clean sweep of the women's events. The Romanians won gold in the pair, four, quad, double and single, and silver in the eight. Canada showed strong behind the dominant Romanians. Tricia Smith and Betty Craig, who had challenged the Romanians in the pair since 1981, won a silver medal. In their first year of rowing the Canadian double together, Silken and Daniele Laumann took bronze. In the single, Andrea missed the bronze by inches. The coxed four won a silver medal.

Pierre de Coubertin, founder of the modern Olympics in 1896, stressed that the Olympic ideal was to be "the best that you can be." He felt sport was a school of moral development for the complete man. (Needless to say, women did not compete in 1896.) The present-day focus is so totally on winning and "gold," however, that anything less can feel like failure, despite a good performance. People watching the women's four receiving their silver medals after the race could not believe the glum faces they wore. The crew did not realize until they were rowing back to the docks that they had raced well. They had to rationalize their way into satisfaction with only silver.

"I knew at the minimum with the four that we were going to get a silver," says Angie Schneider. "We were there because we wanted to be the best in the world. I cherished the silver, but it wasn't the medal I wanted. And it wasn't as good a race as I ever had raced. I believe if you're going to row above yourself, it shouldn't be in a university race for the University of Western Ontario, it should be in an Olympic race." Objectively, it was a very good race. The Canadian women came 2.3 seconds behind the Romanians, who in 1988 are the defending Olympic champions.

In the last race of the day the women's eight placed a bitter and unexpected fourth behind a surprise Dutch crew. The American women won, and the Romanians came second. Unlike the other crews, the women's eight that year had no heats, so they had spent the previous week watching. It's tiring to race, but in a way it's harder to be all set to go with no way to let off steam. They knew they needed help relaxing, focusing. Heather was devastated that she did not make the women's eight, but after their race she thought maybe she was spared a blow. She couldn't think of anything to say to Tina or to her crew. A few months earlier she had shared hopes of a medal with them. Now, anything she said, any gesture made, would seem patronizing.

The eight filed dejectedly up the hill, carrying their boat like a coffin. They walked out of the desert sun and into the tent they shared with eights from other countries, and laid their boat to rest. In the next few moments some of the women clustered together, hugging one another. Others withdrew, trying to find space to hide themselves among the boats, riggers, oars and people. People everywhere. People who didn't belong.

An ill-timed question from a stranger — "How did you do?" — brought from Tina the enraged response — "Fucking fourth." Her crew tried to shush her up, but Tina was too upset. She dropped her oar and repeated, "Fucking fourth again!"

From Tina, the daughter of a missionary, such language was surprising. Understandable, yes. Appropriate, definitely not. The British men's eight was standing a few metres away. They were used to oarswomen swearing, but Princess Anne probably wasn't! And there she was, with her entourage, being introduced to the British athletes.

Rudy came up to Tina after the women's races and said, "Tina, you of all people deserved a medal today." But not everyone always gets her just deserts, and besides, she was looking for a medal, not a hug.

"People didn't feel like they were on par in the crew in 1984," explains Tina. "Some of them thought that they were better than some of the others. And that really hurt the eight, where you're only as fast as you can go together." The problem was compounded because the crew always drove from St. Catharines, where they lived, to Welland, where they trained, with the same people divided between two cars. Three hours of driving a day for three months wore them down. They wanted to complete their workouts as fast as possible. Thus, they discussed the workouts only in the car and understandably came up with different solutions to their problems. Two factions developed, and they never did pull together as one crew.

"We thought that we could have the worst race of our lives and still win a bronze medal," says Tina. "And if we raced really well, we could get a silver. It never occurred to me that I wouldn't come home with an Olympic medal. Some years you have to psych yourself, but this year I really believed it. It was really scary finding ourselves in fifth place and having to row through people to get to fourth. It certainly taught me something about racing. Now I never write any crew off."

Those women in the eight lost status as well as the race by coming fourth that day, especially because their event was very much hurt by the boycott. The Russians and the East Germans were absent, making the field less competitive than when they had come fourth before. But not even the boycott of the Eastern bloc countries could mar the sparkle of the medals. Rudy says, "To this day I have no problem at all with the boycott situation. There are so few Olympics that every country has been to anyway. It's all a relative thing. I spoke to a gentleman who was at the 1932 Games in Los Angeles. He spoke to me at some length about the Canadian eight — a Hamilton Leander eight — that won the bronze in L.A. And I thought, 'Holy shit, that's fantastic, I hope that'll happen to me.' Later on, I looked back in the history books. The irony of the situation was that in 1932, in the eight, there were only three entries. But you know what? He didn't care. He had a bronze medal. Ten years from now, they won't care about the boycott. In 1980 those crews that got medals don't care about the boycott. It's a time and a place."

Tina's race had been one of the two races Heather cared vitally about. The other was the men's eight, in which Heather's friend Kevin Neufeld was racing. On Sunday, the day of the men's finals, Heather tried to watch simultaneously the close-up shots of the men's eight race on the TV monitor and the live race in front of her. But she didn't see much of either because she was too excited. Heather screamed herself hoarse as the sprinting Canadians barely held off the Americans during the last 500 metres of the race.

"It's a pretty incredible feeling, sprinting for the line with 1,500 metres to go," reminisced Kevin afterwards. "I remember wanting to shut it down, and then thinking, 'If you lose this race, you'll never forgive yourself. You'll probably never row well again. Just go, like you've never gone before.' It was a turning point there in that race."

Even with all the preparation there's still the magic of the individual superb performance on the right day. Focus is the essence of performance, and the men had it in their Olympic final. Heather knew the men's eight were champion quality. She believed the crew could pull it off when it mattered. Every guy in that crew, as Kevin said, "had that intensity, that you knew every time no matter what the odds were, that they'd die on the end of the oar before they got beat. And that's the confidence I knew was in the eight."

Heather had known, in her own races, what it was to truly believe she could win, without nursing any doubts. And now she knew it for the eight. When the race was over and she saw Neil Campbell standing apart, tears on his weatherbeaten cheeks, she knew that he had known too. She remembered what Kevin said about Neil: "He's a worker and a fighter. He rowed for Canada in two Olympics, the last one when he was thirty-eight. He knows what it's like to go through the pain. That has a special quality to it." Heather pushed her way through the screaming, jumping crowd to the medal podium a hundred metres away, pulling Kevin's mother with her. Kevin stepped off the podium and hugged Heather, presenting his victor's bouquet to his mother.

When Kevin had stepped off the plane a week earlier in Los Angeles, he had looked like he belonged, with his blond, broad-shouldered Beach Boy looks. And L.A. treated him like a hometown boy. At the Olympics, his dream of winning the Olympic gold came true. Then, after his race, he visited Universal Studios, where he was invited by a stuntman to come back and do movies anytime he wanted to put down his oar.

The Canadian men's eight had tried their mettle at the Lucerne Rotsee Regatta in Switzerland a few weeks before. In the first of two races they had won the gold, beating the American eight by inches. The second day they had lost to the Americans by a similar margin. When the Canadian men's eight got to Los Angeles, they were chomping at the bit to race again. "I remember getting tired of all the work," says Kevin, "because we were ready to race a few weeks before the Olympics. And it's like, okay, let's just get on with it, let's just race. And then I stopped myself and thought, 'Hey, just wait a minute. Remember how many years you've rowed in crummy boats with people you don't like? And now you've got the perfect situation. A bad workout is still a great workout compared to anything else. You really like the people you're rowing with, you're having fun. It's like — enjoy this, not many people get this!'

"Every guy in that crew had that intensity, that you knew every time no matter what the odds were, they'd die on the end of their oar before they got beat. We knew all we had to do was go out there and put the best race we could together. Like Neil says, we were there 'to sneak up, beat the shit out of them, and then leave.' I was in that sense really relaxed, because it didn't really matter if everyone in the world was watching, or how we did, except to do as well as we could.

"For me, the most satisfying thing was after we crossed the line, and seeing the crews we'd beat, and just sitting there in the boat. Even getting the medal wasn't the same. It was like, 'Oh thanks, but I just did what I'm proud of.'" The pageantry of the Olympics meant little to Kevin at the time. He went home the day before the closing ceremonies. Although now, looking back, he says, "I think that maybe I was crazy, missing the closing day. Winning and being part of that doesn't happen that often. But at the time I was thinking, 'Okay, we've won, the Olympics is over, I just want to go home.' The rest is neither here nor there."

Pierre de Coubertin's considered opinion was that women should watch and applaud the victors. In 1984 Heather found herself in that role, not by choice, but by default. It was hard for her not to feel jealous. She hated being left out of anything — and most of all this. To compensate, she lived somewhat vicariously through Kevin. "I would wake up in the night, and remember their race, and feel a rush," recalls Heather. "The euphoria of their experience helped me get through my own disappointment. Still, I often felt like Tina did during the celebrations over the medal performances."

Tina had to gulp down tears of jealousy, watching the others with their medals. To her, the victory in the men's eight was no cause for rejoicing. It only made their own defeat the more bitter. Her way of coming to terms with that fourth place was by withdrawing. She did not want to hear about others' success. In the name of pride and good sportsmanship, the women in the eight wanted to conceal their humiliation. Even though the men and women don't race each other, they establish an unstated pecking order within the national team subculture on the basis of performance.

After the races, the rowers left Lake Casitas, rode two and a half hot sweaty hours in the bus down to Los Angeles and stayed at the University of Southern California. There, they got free tickets to watch any events they wanted. At the USC campus, there were thousands of people who were stars. They were getting a lot more recognition than the rowers were, since they were from higher-profile sports and were individual celebrities already. That helped to bring things back into perspective for the rowers. But at the same time, people would still reach out and try to touch the medallists.

Angie rejoiced in her women's four silver with the same single-mindedness she'd applied to the earning of the medal. While Kevin thought the race itself was the only important thing, Angie thought the medal embodied the race and the pain. "I was overwhelmed at the time with the trappings of victory," she says.

"There are people out there who manage to be humble, but I'm not one of them," says Angie. The Olympics mattered so much to her. It was a dream come true. She is from a small town deep in tobacco country, where dreams don't put food on the table. Because of her interest in sport, Angie got to university, started in physical education and then fastened on philosophy as her academic love. A natural athlete, she came into rowing from track and field in 1979 when she was twenty. She started trying out for the national team in 1981, finally making the top crew in the year it mattered.

"The medals I got in sport — and this isn't the case anymore because I no longer need to prove anything there, so it's an interesting comparison — they symbolized the effort I'd put into it and the accomplishment. I'd hang them up on the wall. When people came in they'd see them and what I had achieved. And the Olympics — that was the *crème de la crème,* the Nobel Prize of athletics. I went to a banquet after the races, in Los Angeles, and thousands of people were there, asking for my autograph. It took a long time to adjust to it, but it's hard to give it up. You get the highest highs from all this admiration. It's like you're on a boat, and the water comes and pulls you up and away, and you're just carried along."

Banquet followed banquet in the fall of 1984 as Canada rejoiced over the fine performances of its medal-winning athletes. Yet Jane Tregunno, who stroked the women's four, found that dissatisfaction with her silver medal had not confined itself to the moment on the podium. As girlfriend of Blair Horn, the stroke man in the gold medal eight, she got as much attention for *that* "achievement" as she did for her medal. Jane is a golden-girl who, it seems, effortlessly gathers the laurels for her crown. From a "good family," she had the resulting poise — until she discovered that as a woman medallist people treated her differently from her male counterparts.

Jane was jolted into awareness of her lesser importance at a dinner for the Olympians at Ridley College in St. Catharines. All the medallists who had rowed for the Ridley Grad Boat Club attended.

"I was at the Ridley banquet with my family," says Jane, "to be honoured together with the men's eight and a member of the men's quad who had won a bronze medal. I was one of two athletes there who had graduated from Ridley College. Like the other athletes, I was a member of the Ridley Grad Boat Club. But I was virtually ignored when they were handing out the awards. Granted, I hadn't won a gold medal, but I felt like a silver medal didn't mean anything to them at all. Then my brother-in-law stood up. He had graduated from Ridley too. 'What about Jane Tregunno?' he shouted. Normally I would have been a little embarrassed, but I was so angry at being overlooked that I was glad to have him speak up."

Heather discovered that her status as gold medal girlfriend blotted out her status as athlete. She attended a banquet as a member of the Olympic team but was elevated to a special table as a guest of the honoured gold medal winners. A well-meaning but idiotic woman gushed, "It must have been such an experience for you, dear, to be able to go to the Olympics to watch your boyfriend race!" Heather cringed. She never quite knew which was worse. As an Olympic athlete herself, did she want to explain her private humiliation of being team alternate? In her sixth year on the national team, she had let herself down, badly. That offered little relief.

But the medal winners felt on top of the world. It was an emotional release — in the previous year they'd just been building and building. And in addition, there was so much hype surrounding the Olympics.

Winning lights up the world. Suddenly people in the crew that the athletes previously only tolerated become special best friends. Their presence gives a thrill like the thrill of sharing ecstasy with a lover. Although fellow crewmates may have nothing in common with each other save the race, they have shared the freedom and communion of absolute physicality. Together they triumphed and created the world. Succeeding like that is a proud experience. Whether or not others are happy with their performance does not touch them. They are untouchable. The triumphant bubble within feels like it will never burst.

TV interviewers encourage the smiling medallists to talk about all the sacrifices they have made to "get to the top," to reach this wonderful moment of appearing on screens across the nation. Is that a technique aimed at the viewer, to make the athlete seem more human because he or she has problems too? Is this the only way the twentieth century can stomach its heroes — by taking them flawed but gutsy? At least that way everyone can be the little matchgirl warming her hands on the fires of achievement — the achievement that can come to anyone who believes in it enough, works hard enough. It is not a large jump from there to thinking that their victory means they worked harder than all the other athletes did. In fact, this rationale is a powerful psychological tool that athletes employ to convince themselves they can win. And it's an even smaller jump from there to thinking that because they worked harder, and won, they are more worthy people. They cannot help thinking that in some sense they passed a test other people failed. In that special way others are lesser than they, the winners. Intellectually they can understand that last time they did, or next time they might, lose. But in victory they are invincible. In victory they gain credibility as athletes. It is easy to translate that sense of credibility as athletes into a sense of worth as people.

The intense focusing on the single goal of the Olympics colours other aspects of athletes' lives. Anything that does not bear directly upon performance becomes irrelevant. Athletes do not care to chat about the weather for the sake of polite small-talk, no matter how much such a conversation might mean to the other person. But if suddenly the weather might affect their performance, then it becomes a topic of passionate significance and is considered obsessively as it relates to them. This loss of proportion happens even to those athletes who try to balance their lives, since by its nature high-performance sport demands total commitment. For those who lost, regaining their sense of self-worth is a difficult task. For the winners, regaining a sense of the real self is almost as hard.

When Angie came home after the Olympics, a welcoming committee was waiting at the airport in London, Ontario. The friend whose family she was staying with for a week was there to pick her up, along with reporters from the local TV station. Together they watched the passengers file out of the plane. Angie appeared at last. She paused at the top of the steps, her silver medal glinting on her chest. She descended majestically, smiling, and walked across the tarmac. And was deluged with questions from the press.

"What was it like?"

"How did it feel?"

"What is the significance of the silver medal looking like it does?"

Proudly, Angie explained that the pink, mint green and gold of the tricolour ribbon were chosen because they were not used in any country's flag. The medal had been designed by Pierre de Coubertin in 1896; it showed a flowery relief of Greek victors being carried aloft by a cheering crowd. Her friend, a rower who had not made the national team and who could not bear to go to L.A. and watch the Olympics, sat on the grass and waited, full of conflicting emotions. She was proud of Angie for pulling herself up by her bootstraps, but she resented the self-centredness and envied the success.

Angie had the "right stuff" by the world's definition in August of 1984. Looking back now, she says, "I wanted to hang on to that special feeling so much, at the time, because I put everything I had into it. I was ruthless at that stage and in a dream world — the fantasy surreal world of the Olympics." Until she broke out of seeing things that way, she would not realize that she was not a superwoman. But before she did so, she was lost in her dreamworld. All she wanted to do was rest, and smile, and look at her medal. She was dreaming about an Olympic lover. Olympic medallists (as opposed even to regular Olympians) were a superior breed of athlete, she confided to her friend. They also were the only group from which she could think of selecting a partner at that point. Fortuitously, she had met a suitable man at the Olympics — and there had been instant fire between them.

One afternoon, a few days after Angie came to London, the phone rang. It was for her. When she hung up, she wafted around the house on an almost visible pink cloud. Her Olympic lover was coming, driving across the country from California to New York. He was making a special trip up to London to see her. Another fantasy had survived into the real world!

The weather was brutally hot and sultry. A storm was brewing. Such a storm it was, too! The sky turned green and purple, the lightning flashed pink. Best of all, the electricity went out. Around ten o'clock, the family was playing cards by candlelight when the phone rang. It was He. He was in a gas station just off the 401 and wanted to know how to get to the house. Someone gave him directions, and they prepared for his arrival in the next half hour.

Angie prepared in a way that took the rest of them rather aback. First she slipped upstairs and changed into a tight black dress. Then she announced that she would stand at the end of the driveway and wait for him. The driveway is very long and its entrance obscure even at the best of times. But with all the city lights out the blackness verged on inky. Did Angie want a flashlight? No, she thought she would prefer to do without. She would take the candelabra and guide him in that way. To this day, no one but Angie knows whether the candles stayed lit in the strong wind or how many random passers-by went off the road in surprise. But the dream man arrived.

4

POLITICS AND PASSION

Angie acknowledges that "the medal did go to my head, just from being there. The hierarchy's created like that. But look what they do with the people that win! They put you on firetrucks for parades through town, they give you the world. And the person who gets fourth, gets nothing. We believed there was nothing we couldn't do, in anything — intellectually, too. That medal meant success anywhere. 'Doors open, curriculum vitaes — here it is,' said Rudy."

Their Olympic medals gave the rowers a brief taste of celebrity status, especially the gold medal of the men's eight — the gold stands apart in its glory. But in general the sport of rowing dwells apart from the hype of publicity. Indeed, rowers take pride in the fact that they work their brains out and devote themselves to a task where the only reward is the intrinsic value of performing well. It's part of the gentlemanly rowing culture — of being an amateur, committing oneself for love alone, rejoicing in the personal challenge.

The sport of rowing in Canada attracts very few. All told about 8,000 people row competitively. Some 40 per cent of them are women. That the rowing population is small is in itself hardly upsetting. The majority of Olympic sports are in a similar position. Not very many people fence or own kayaks. On the whole, rowers do not regret their low profile.

After the 1984 Olympics, someone who is used to marketing sport said that all the members of the men's eight could have
been millionaires if they'd marketed themselves properly. All of
them doubtless benefited from the gold's presence on their
resumes. "But if you win," Kevin Neufeld, who was in that crew,
responded, "you don't want it, you don't really want or need
that stuff. I remember just the look on our crew's faces in a press
conference after our race. Everyone looked a little embarrassed.
We knew why we were there, but we weren't used to it. I think
that if you're in rowing for the glory, you're not going to be in
it for long. The glory doesn't take away from what you did, but
it doesn't add to it. The competition was *it*. Whether it be getting together with Neil, our coach, and the guys and watching
the videotape of the race again — that's part of it too. The other
part is fun, but that's that."

The number of people who compete in a sport non-competi-
tively relates directly to the sport's marketability. In Canada,
only 3 per cent of Canadian athletes enjoy sport-related income
apart from government assistance. Skiers are particularly noted
for balancing the dual role of athlete and entrepreneur. A top
skier, like Canadian Rob Boyd, may sign a contract with a ski
equipment sponsor that promises, on top of a base salary, a
$50,000 to $100,000 bonus for a World Cup win. The top earner
in skiing previous to the 1988 Winter Olympics, Luxembourg's
Marc Giradelli, nets $2 million a year. The International Ski
Federation allows athletes to retain Olympic eligibility if the national body puts the money in a trust fund. The World Cup skiing
circuit is a $200- to $300-million-a-year industry. Since that
amount of money is there, it is right and proper that the athletes
get a piece of the pie.

To save its life, rowing could not compete against the alpine
ski team for corporate dollars. Thousands of TV viewers see Ros-
signol plastered all over World Cup skis and buy the same brand
for themselves. Those same TV viewers will not rush out to buy
rowing shells, because they don't row on Sunday afternoons.
Lesley Thompson, who coxed the silver medal women's four at

the 1984 Olympics and won bronze medals in 1985 and 1986 as well, discovered in 1986 that Canadian Tire Corporation planned to sponsor an athlete. Being a good businesswoman, she presented herself to them as an example of athletic excellence and also as the daughter of a senior member of the corporation.

"Canadian Tire chose a female skier," says Lesley. "She had won fewer medals than I had. But because she was a skier and I was a rower, she got it. I resent somewhat that I cannot market my athletic excellence in the corporate world."

On the whole, though, rowers are almost glad that rowing has a low profile. The media and financial pressure in other sports put great pressure on the athletes. Such pressures distort the amateur's pleasure of sport for its own sake. But rowers know the pressure of insufficient funds, as Rowing Canada looks long and hard for corporate sponsors.

"For press coverage, or to be known walking down the street, well, if you're looking for that, then you're in the wrong sport anyway," says Doug Hamilton, Olympic medallist and 1985 World champion in the men's quad. "Peer respect is the most important. The peers know that your performance depends on the quality of the event in a year, the competition. They also understand the self-sacrifice involved, how hard it is to get there. I suppose it depends where you want to get your gratitude — from the peer who knows the value, or from the girl in the singles' bar, who's most impressed by the Olympics and the gold."

In 1984 the rowers got lots of non-peer gratitude from a very impressed Liberal government. As the brand-new heroes in August 1984, all Olympic medallists were invited to a gala reception at the Canadian National Exhibition grounds in Toronto, hosted by the then prime minister, John Turner. The Liberal Party was at an all-time low ebb of confidence and popularity. Pierre Trudeau, its leader for so many years, had just stepped down in June. Welcoming home the victorious Olympians was a happy task for Turner, who was in the unenviable position of nursing the minority Liberal government through to the September election. The athletes' success in Los Angeles was in many ways the result of the Canadian government's decision to pour millions of dollars into developing high-performance sport. It was a high-profile Liberal success story, so the Liberals made much of it. But it took the athletes by surprise.

"Someone phoned me up from the Prime Minister's Office and said could I come, they'd send down a cab for me," recalls Kevin. "I said, 'No, it's okay, I'll catch a ride with our coxswain.' And they said, 'Well, we'll give you gas money.' I said fine, and then we drove to Toronto and I got to our hotel room and there were two guys from our eight. And I was, like, 'What are you guys doing here?' And right then, I sort of clued in to what people really thought of all this. I thought, 'People are spending thousands of dollars to have us here in Toronto' — for what to me was just an insignificant little event. It was very foreign to us, although we got used to it. I don't know whether that was good or bad. You forget what got you there."

We've all heard the myth that sport and politics don't mix. Right from the start, however, Pierre de Coubertin's interest in reviving the Olympic movement was motivated by national self-interest. His idea of an Olympics stemmed from a campaign to include sport in France's school curriculum. His emphasis on the place of sport grew from his feeling that Germany's defeat of France in the Franco-Prussian War in 1871 resulted partly from the poor physical condition of France's people. He tried to prevent Germany from competing in the first Olympiad in 1896, since it was the historic enemy of his country.

Both host and participating countries have political pride at stake in the Olympic Games. The International Olympic Committee picks the host city that it believes will mount the best Games. That sounds apolitical until one realizes that the country uses the Olympics to its advantage. The Berlin Games in 1936 are ridiculed today because Hitler used them to highlight the Third Reich's Aryan superiority. The Americans auctioned out the 1984 Games to corporate sponsors, and when that was wildly successful, attributed the success to capitalism and the

"American Way." In 1988 Korea is getting a lot of mileage out of advertising its economic miracle via the Olympic publicity.

The Olympic Games are political in their very nature, since they organize athletes by countries. The medal count is linked to the worth of the political system of each country. The media talks about "winning" and "losing" nations, not athletes. It plays off the number of medals the Easties have against the number of medals the democratic countries of the West have. Eastern bloc countries are accused of using their athletes to trumpet the success of socialism. In capitalist societies, however, the Games have been known to perpetuate class distinctions. In 1948 the Swedish dressage team lost its gold medal when it was found out that one of the members was a non-commissioned officer, although all the members were career army men. Commissioned officers qualified as amateurs; other ranks did not.

The Games have long been a tool for international reward and punishment. In 1948 the first postwar Olympics were held in London, England, and the Germans, Italians and Japanese were not invited. Countries swell with righteous pride over the Olympics and dictate who can come to the party, but the individual athlete is the one who pays the price. Athletes, not countries, were devastated when the threatened boycott of the Moscow Olympics became a reality in 1980. What hurt most for the Canadian athletes was that the government did not also impose economic sanctions. Canada seemed not to be really interested in standing up to the Soviet invasion of Afghanistan, but just in aping the Americans. Without grain embargoes, the boycott was just a ritual slap in the face.

Tricia, Andrea, Lesley, Jane and Heather were on the national team that did not go to Moscow in 1980. Tricia and Andrea both may have forfeited a medal by not going that year. But generally they were luckier than most because, by Seoul, they will have had two more shots at Olympic medals. For many oarswomen on the 1980 team, that was their final chance. Inexperienced at the Montreal Olympics in 1976, they had had three successful years of World Championship competition to prepare them for Moscow in 1980. Because many were in their mid-twenties in 1980, they were peaking physically. They really had something to lose by not going. And they were very upset. Enclosed as they were in their world of weights, runs and rows, the outer world seemed awfully irrelevant. Still, it made decisions about their future.

The black nations boycotted the Commonwealth Games in Edinburgh in 1986. They wanted to protest the Thatcher government's policy of not imposing economic sanctions on South Africa. South African athletes already are not allowed to compete in international games because of their government's apartheid policy. And it is Sport Canada's policy that Canadian athletes who compete with South Africans be banned from further competition.

In July 1986 Heather had her birthday and her race in the double at the Commonwealth Games within two days — good reasons to get mail. She was elated one day to find a telegram. Her teammates gathered around in excitement and something akin to jealousy because she had got mail and they hadn't. When athletes compete overseas, one of the few links they have with the outside world is mail. Most athletes ritually check the hotel desk to see if they've gotten any. When Heather opened the envelope, the smile left her face. "Who's it from?" people asked. "Just someone back home — no big deal," Heather said as she turned away. Neither a birthday nor good luck greeting, the message was from sports historian and activist Bruce Kidd. As a former athlete he knew the price he was asking Heather to pay when he requested her to "urge all Canadian athletes to boycott the Games to show solidarity with black athletes."

Heather was opposed to governments paternalistically imposing boycotts upon the athletes, but this was different. In this situation, she herself could choose whether to take that political stand. Athletes make great personal sacrifices for what they believe in, or they wouldn't be at the Games at all; Heather, though, usually preferred to look at her commitment to excellence in sport as choice rather than as sacrifice. But this time she saw clearly that the choice about her values meant sacrifice. Did she value the ideal of sport transcending politics more than she valued the opportunity that sport might give her to speak out against apartheid? The question perplexed Heather but she chose to be pragmatic about it. The Canadian rowers were staying in Glasgow. They were hours away from all the other athletes, who were staying in Edinburgh. Secondly, as it was the night before their races, they already had entered their own world of race preparation.

"I decided that one athlete making a statement about apartheid would not make any noise. Especially a low-profile athlete like myself. And furthermore, my choice not to compete would force my double partner not to compete too. If the athletes had, as a group, decided to back it, it might have been effective. But anyway, I wasn't so sure it would support the black athletes. They too wanted to compete. I had seen the Bermudan athletes at the opening ceremonies, since their letter, 'B,' was right before us as Canadians. We had stood outside the stadium together waiting for our turn to enter, and we could see the change of expression on their faces as the decision about their participation was made and changed several times in a few moments. It was really poignant. We felt such solidarity with them, knowing how much they wanted to compete and knowing that they might not be allowed. They came in at the end, out of alphabetical order, and everyone in the stadium cheered for them. But then we heard a few days later that their government had changed its mind, and they had had to leave."

Discovering that they are pawns in political games tarnishes some athletes' naive patriotic sense that Canada has high and pure aspirations. If they thought about it, though, athletes would realize that they serve a function for the government. Athletes represent their country, and the government hopes to get value for the money it puts into sport. By rising to the top of their sport, world-class athletes demonstrate that they are winners in at least one area. Canada basks in these celebrities' reflected glory and applies their credibility to as many ends as possible.

"My brother-in-law thinks rowers are taking the government's money to do this, like welfare," says Jane Tregunno. In theory, carding (the assistance given by Sport Canada) is meant to supplement other sources of income, but 70 per cent of athletes in Canada are entirely dependent upon their $450 per month. Sport hovers uneasily between being seen as useful to society and being seen as the self-indulgence of the young. If athletes are just doing sport to satisfy their egos, after all, why should taxpayers support them? But the Canadian government demonstrated its belief that sport was useful when in 1972 it founded Sport Canada, the branch of the Fitness and Amateur Sport Ministry that administers high-performance sport. When the International Olympic Committee dropped the stipulation that athletes be "amateur" in 1974, Canada had little choice but to play ball by international sport standards if it cared to produce competitive athletes. It did. The sport system was extended to find and develop Canadian talent, as well as fund it. For the government to fund athletes was viewed as radical twenty years earlier, but by the late 1980s Sport Canada was kicking in $57 million a year to that end. However, with no gold at the Calgary Olympics, the expenditures are being called into question. It is a sign of how arbitrary the expectations are that *only* gold medals could validate government spending despite Canada's strongest Winter Olympic showing ever — more top-ten finishers than ever before. After the Calgary Games were over, Otto Jelinek, the then minister of fitness and amateur sport, complained that today's athletes are spoon-fed, and harkened back to his own days of competition. People would do well to remember that despite these big expenditures, the athletes themselves still receive only $450 a month. It's hard for athletes to make a full-time commitment with so little financial support. But the pressure is there for them to do so. Coaches Laurent Roux and Marty Hall said, after the performances of the Canadian cross-country ski team at the Calgary Olympics, that the program is going to get tougher and demand more commitment from athletes. As quoted in the *Globe and Mail* on February 29, 1988, they said skiing "has to be their lives."

In the 1980s Canadian national team rowers train at high-performance sport centres, where their improvement is monitored by five professional coaches. Rowing Canada, the national organization, has five people on staff in Ottawa and hundreds of dedicated volunteers at the club level across the country. Rowing Canada, like other national sport organizations, is reorganizing itself. It has just recently changed its name from the century-old Canadian Amateur Rowing Association. The loss of the amateur designation is a sign of the times, but the organization still has the same mandate — to organize national regattas, encourage the formation of provincial associations and clubs, set regatta rules and organize the national team. Some 4,000 people in some sixty clubs are registered with Rowing Canada, while an additional 4,000 row unregistered. In the 1980s, with the increased emphasis on high-performance sport, Rowing Canada has acted more and more as liaison between Sport Canada and the rowing membership.

Canada is known in some circles as the Western world's East Germany because of the state's extensive involvement in amateur sport.

"To my knowledge, the Canadian system is somewhere between the Romanian and the American — some government support and some self-support," says Romanian Valeria Recila. Valeria won the gold medal in the single sculls at the 1984 Olympics. Later, she married a Dutch oarsman, and for 1988 is training in the Netherlands. "In Eastern Europe the state provides more support than governments do in the West. Sport is a normal thing for people to do and get paid in Romania. If athletes want to study they can, but it's not possible to hold a job. For rowing, we trained a lot, too much to work. It took seven hours a day from January to after the World Championships.

"In Romania athletes are admired. Sport is special there just as it is anywhere in the world. To do sports you need your talents."

"Ben Johnson, doing what he's doing for Canadians in Rome, is probably worth more than a dozen delegations of high-power diplomats," said then Minister of Sport Otto Jelinek. The sprinter achieved international renown by setting the world record in the 100-metre sprint at the World Athletics Championships in August 1987. Hot on the heels of Jelinek's comment, External Affairs Minister Joe Clark announced in October 1987 that Sport Canada would set up an international relations division to keep athletes aware of federal policies so that they could actively represent their country at diplomatic functions.

By being a winner, Johnson personifies victory and youth and a masterful orientation to challenges. He projects a positive image of Canada internationally and at home. He is a hero because he is pushing back a definable limit of humankind's ability by being the fastest man ever. Clark and Jelinek wanted to piggyback on Johnson's success and catch some reflected glory. Sport, unlike politics, is simple — the winning there is easy to identify and appreciate. Despite being simple, though, it means something. As one athlete says, "We pour our lives into it." Each time athletes go out and win a race, they feel as if they have triumphed on a symbolic as well as a physical level because they have pitted their will against the unknown. People identify with sport because the happy ending is possible. They celebrate the winner without feeling too bad about the loser. Athletes know that "in a race the worst to fear is that you'll lose and it'll be horrible. But you won't die."

Like Ben Johnson, all athletes provide living examples of the archetypal struggle of the individual against the environment. Whether their environment is the racecourse or the gym, they have still set themselves a task and striven to achieve it. Athletes refuse to give up in the face of adversity; they stop only when the game is over. If the game is close, it is that much more powerful, just as struggle before any victory makes the triumph mean more. Likewise, defeated athletes redeem themselves if they demonstrate the human spirit's dignity against insuperable odds. Athletes are heroes in much the same way that all people who risk themselves to gain a personal goal are heroes. And their heroism too is sung. The coxswain of the women's eight piped the theme song from the movie *Flashdance* through the boat before the race in Lucerne in 1983: "Take your passion, make it happen," ran the words. Corny, yes, but athletes really do live by that sentiment.

Kay Worthington has been trying to make her passion happen since 1981, the first year she was on the national team. She rowed in the eight from 1981 until 1984 and met frustration at the World Championships each year — a good but disappointing fourth-place finish in 1981, when the eight was new and untried; fifth in 1982, after which she spearheaded the effort to throw out Rudy; and fourth again in 1983. The fourth-place finish at the 1984 Olympics was the last straw. "It made me look at myself and say, 'Is this true?' I spent more time crying in the summer of 1984 than I had in my whole life before that. We were faster in May than in July at the Olympics. We got slower because of the frustration. I felt so ripped off. After such an experience, you have to say we were responsible, because we were out there racing. A coach writes the training program, and you can only do what you want inside that, but you still have to do that. You have to come to peace with yourself and explain what happened. But I came to the point where I realized 'it's not me, it can't be me.' The only way to control your situation, I remember telling a track-and-field coach after our race, is to eliminate the variables. An eight had the most variables — ten people were involved in getting you from A to B as fast as possible."

Kay had reached the point where she had either to quit or create a situation in which she personally could perform. When she switched from sweep to sculling that fall, she chose a heroic path. She bent rowing to her will, deciding she "would be independent and still be on the team." In 1985 she made the quad. But she knew she had to find a better training environment than her native Toronto if she wanted to achieve her potential as a sculler.

"In Toronto," complains Kay, "my whole experience was one of isolation. And besides that, the water stinks and getting to and from the boathouse is a pain. Those things weighed heavily on me. It was just easier to run and do weights, and not row. A friend of mine on the U.S. team, Mike Teti, would phone me and say jokingly, 'When are you coming to Philadelphia?' The idea grew on me, more than I cared to admit. The attraction of having the boathouses and perfect water that close was enormous. And there really wasn't any place that I liked in all aspects for living and training in Canada. In Vancouver it was such a hassle to drive from the city to Burnaby Lake that I wasn't keen when I went out to train. I wanted it to be over as soon as possible. As a city, Victoria was too slow moving for me. Going to Philly a couple of times in the spring of '85, I thought, 'Wow, this is really cool.' Twelve boathouses all in a row. When you stand on the dock at about 3 p.m. and you watch all the boats come out of the boathouses, you think that everyone in America rows."

In 1985, when she was twenty-five, Kay was ready to commit herself to one path, although she was still not certain what. She started law school that fall. By Christmas, she had decided what she would do. She left law school so that she could go to Philadelphia and concentrate on training. When she got there, she realized, "I couldn't have set up a better situation if I had dreamed it. It was such a feeling, to have a really competitive training environment. I wanted that. And support. From Mike and from all the rowers. You want to go where you have the most support. That kind of support is great."

In 1986 Kay tried out for and made that year's top boat, the quad. But once again her high hopes were frustrated when injuries of two of the athletes prevented the crew from racing at the World Championships. Being victimized one more time by the variables of a crew "fuelled my desire to be in the single — just wanting to be in control." In a happy ending, she won the single trials at the 1987 selection race in Welland in May. Yet her struggles continued. In June Kay got a call from Jim Joy, Rowing Canada's high-performance director, saying she had to train in Canada for the rest of the summer or she would be decarded. He felt that as the Canadian sculler, she should be based in Canada. If she stayed in Philadelphia, he said, she could still go to the World Championships, but at her own expense.

Government-financed high-performance sport sets up a *quid pro quo* between government and athlete. Athletes sign contracts with their national sport organizations. The contracts, though differing from sport to sport, are based on a generic contract put together by Sport Canada. Prior to 1985 there was no contract, although athletes were still carded on the same basis as they are now — on their performance and the recommendation of Sport Canada. According to the contract, athletes must live in an environment conducive to high-performance sport, attend mandatory events like training camps and national championships, and follow the national team training program. They must follow a certain code of conduct, which can include not speaking to the media without the permission of their national sport organization. Athletes must reach certain performance objectives to get their carding. The national sport organization must set out the selection procedures for the national team in advance.

Each sport sets different sorts of conditions for the athletes. High-profile sports put more conditions on when and how athletes can speak to the media. The alpine skiing contract is very fat — it looks like a contract between employer and employee. Diving, where the athletes are younger, has rules governing sightseeing, shopping and dating. Rowing, with a much older group of athletes, does not have a prescribed code of conduct.

Rowing is one of the few sports where the contract is negotiated. The Athletes' Council in rowing felt that if the contract is indeed between two equal parties — the athlete and Rowing Canada — then the athletes should help draft it. The athletes suggested some changes in the clauses but as of early 1988 had not received an answer. In protest, the more activist rowers are encouraging all the carded rowers to refuse to sign the annual contract. At the time of writing, the situation is at a standstill. In rowing, the disputed issue is principally how many training camps are mandatory, since the athletes are reluctant to take what they consider unnecessary time off work. The athletes dislike the wide-open stipulation that they "dedicate themselves wholeheartedly to their sport." How, they ask, can anyone measure who "tries hardest"? They object to being told that they have to do everything a certain way *and* get a certain result. Their level of carding, which translates into the amount of money they get, is based on their performance. Athletes feel that they should have freedom of choice as long as they produce. They also feel that being asked to limit their autonomy for $450 to $650 a month, which is very hard to live on, is unreasonable. The demand that athletes live in an environment conducive to high-performance sport is also dangerously nebulous, as Kay found out in the fuss over her residence in Philadelphia.

"The contractual agreement of carding forces you to do things you don't want to do," rages Kay. "I know in some ways the more organized system is good. There are more informed coaches around, more money. But the Canadian structure is very paternalistic. In the U.S. you have your freedom off the water, although on the water you submit, while in Canada you are a peon, almost. I know we have one-tenth the population the Americans do, so per capita we do far better than they do. I know the American athletes have to scrounge. But I was forced to pick up my whole life and leave everything on hold.

"It seems that in Canada there is the feeling that if you have x input, you will have a gold medal output, by virtue of Sport Canada. That's no better than what they criticize the Eastern bloc for." Kay could not risk being decarded because at the time she did not have the papers that would allow her to work in the States. She had to return to Canada and had difficulty adjusting her training. She tried for a while to live at her parents' house in Toronto but was miles away from facilities. Ultimately she worked out a satisfactory situation in St. Catharines.

"It was bad enough leaving Philly!" says Kay. "In Philly there was so much support. It seemed like every single person I'd ever met wanted to know how I was doing when I went down to get my stuff when I moved to Canada. People were yelling to me as they rowed by me — 'Kay, how'd you do? They're forcing you to go back? Oh my God!' Everyone knew what my situation was."

Kay roomed with Heather Clarke and Jane Tregunno at the Rotsee Regatta in Lucerne in July. She shocked them with her reports of the problems she had trying to get there. The Rotsee is the major international race before the World Championships. It acts as a testing ground for crews to see how they compare before they meet at the Worlds. In Lucerne, while other crews were being led by their coaches through the rituals of the pre-race week, Kay had been on her own. She had no coach, and she was waiting for her racing shell to arrive. Jane and Heather had thought at first that she thrived on the challenge, even though she made self-deprecating jokes.

"Wouldn't it be a laugh if after all this I didn't even make the finals?" she said. The other two knew Kay was fast; they knew how hard she'd trained during the year. They had heard of her successful races against American scullers and had seen her beat Silken Laumann in the single trials. They also knew that Kay demanded much of herself and seemed to have a pre-race ritual of self-doubt. Thus, despite the words, initially Heather and Jane were confident that Kay would channel all her energy to her advantage.

Then Kay got really upset the day before the race. "How can they expect me to perform?" she burst out. "I didn't even know until a few days ago that I'd be coming?"

Jane and Heather looked at Kay, horrified. "What do you mean?" they asked in unison.

"They left my name off the list of people going to the regatta, so I didn't get any information or a plane ticket. I just found out by chance that it was this weekend, so I phoned to find out where my ticket was. That's why I was on a different flight from you guys."

"I thought you were on a different flight because you came from Philadelphia," said Heather.

"Hah!" snorted Kay with typical vehemence. "I wish!"

But Kay raced heroically in Lucerne. She won two bronze medals, one on each day of the finals. She beat Valeria Recila, the defending Olympic champion. The resilience she showed in getting back on track after her setbacks was exemplary. Kay attributed maintaining her focus to "those friends being so supportive. When I went out on the water in Lucerne, I felt nervous but relaxed. I saw familiar faces, and I knew they cared how I did. That made a world of difference."

Kay is willing to be the athlete-hero who pursues excellence for the love of it alone, she is willing to suffer financial hardship, but she needs to hear the feedback telling her what she's doing is worthwhile. "In Canada it seemed like so few people cared about my performance. But maybe that's because the Americans like their celebrities. I think it's significant that there's no Hollywood in Canada, whereas it expresses an American mentality."

Athletes express physical striving and the ecstasy found through it. At its best, high-performance sport is an art form, by Plato's definition of art. Both performers and participants experience an emotional release, a catharsis. But more than the performance arts, sport suffers from a bad reputation. The physical is demeaned because it is, by Plato's grade, the "lowest" sense. However, the celebration of the physical does not imply that this is the only level people should operate on. And although athletes strive for victory in a race, they know that in other areas competing may be inappropriate or even morally wrong.

The problem with seeing sport as allegorical to life is that people may fail to distinguish the allegory from the reality of life. Ronald Reagan goes too far when he says that life is like the Super Bowl. On their part, too, athletes must stay aware that sport goes only so far. One member of the women's four, Barb Armbrust, observed that "for four years, I've been a hero. With the Calgary Olympics, there are now a whole new set of heroes. It'll be really interesting to see how people from 1984 react to maybe not being heroes in the next Olympic session. Maybe we'll realize we've been walking around thinking we're special. I don't feel like I've been thinking like that, but maybe I have."

"Through rowing," says Angie, "we get to romanticize our lives — and also death." For her, life and death had met when her pair partner's mother died in 1981. "The crossover of the fantasy world of sport with such a reality changed my whole appreciation of what both meant." Using the vocabulary of life and death in the pre-race psych-up process is effective. Kevin gave his 1984 crewmates the highest of all accolades when he said they would "die on the end of the oar before they got beat." Angie and Heather's varsity coach at Western said to "take no prisoners." Doug Clark, Heather and Tina's first coach, said to "go flat out 'til you pass out." But there comes a time when the line should perhaps be drawn so that sport does not become life or death. A freshman at Harvard finished the last three minutes of an ergometer test while his nose rhythmically spurted blood down his shirt. His coach did not stop him because he wanted to see if the boy was tough. Then and there the boy earned the respect of all his crewmates by demonstrating so graphically that he would put it all on the line for rowing. In 1986 the Russian men's pair, the Pimenov brothers, showed what the will to win could cost. They had been World champions for eight years. That year, the British men's pair gave them a race to the end. The Pimenovs won by inches, but the bowman passed out at the line and had to be rushed to the hospital. All rowers would say, and mean it, "That's not wrong, if what you are there for is to win."

When you really want to make it, you don't see the boundaries limiting the importance of sport. You see succeeding by that measure as the sole purpose of your life, as Angie did for a time. Angie, who competed at five feet eleven inches and 170 pounds, is a talented and naturally strong athlete. She was convinced from the start that rowing was "my way of proving my worth." Coming from Rodney, Ontario, Angie felt, "I needed to achieve in that area because I'm not from that elite, and I wanted it. It was the way I would crawl out of my position. Since sport had always been there, I thought, 'This is my gift, my method of expression.'"

Angie had no idea what it would take to realize her goal. The first time she tried out for the national team she didn't make it, but she bounced back pretty easily. The second time it almost killed her. In the 1982 selection, Angie says, "I knew when I went in to see Rudy what he would say, although I didn't admit it to myself. He put down the points. I had done really well on the erg, and okay in the Speed Order and the seat-racing — all the objective tests. So I didn't do too badly in those three categories, but I got killed in the subjective ones, because as far as they were concerned I had no compatibility. I think I got zero on compatibility, out of ten." For Angie, "it was like 1981, I was the last person again. And I freaked out on Rudy. I pounded my fist on the table and said, 'What the hell do I have to do to make this goddam team?' And he looked at me, and I think it was the first time he thought that I took it seriously. Before that, I think he thought it was a plaything to me. And he said something which I remembered for a long time. He said, 'Angela, I will guarantee, I will do everything except put it in writing, that you will be on the 1984 Olympic team.'

"But I was devastated. I went into shock. I hurt so badly, and my perception was so skewed, so focused on this thing, and this thing had failed me, that my life, for me, was over. It's astounding to look back on now. How terrifying to have your life determined by a man, whether you think you should live or die. You give him all the power when you undertake this thing. I thought, 'My God, this is it, I've put everything in my life into this and now I won't make it.'" While objectively Angie had a lot going on in her life aside from rowing, she couldn't see it that way. Even when her mother tried to get her to evaluate her situation, "it was like an anorexic. You take her to the mirror and show her her body and say, 'You're not fat, you're thin.' And she looks at herself, and says, 'No, you're wrong.' It just didn't register."

In 1983 Angie was on the line once again. "I was at home between races on the last day, resting. Rudy had called me over and told me my neck was on the line that morning. I was so nervous I wasn't sleeping, and my stomach was bothering me. I called home and my dad answered the phone. I was a complete wreck — for me it was life or death. I don't think Dad knew that, but he knew it was making the team or not. My dad is a really good and confident athlete. He said, 'It's like golf. First, you have to stop focusing on all those things happening around you and distracting your attention. When I go to drive the tee, I can't focus on what will happen and what those people will think of me if the ball falls off, because if you lose your concentration, for sure it will happen. Just pretend you're the only person in the world doing it, and it's for yourself. Make everything simple, just go do it, have fun, and enjoy yourself.' He brought me back to earth and reality. I went that afternoon and creamed everybody. And because of that, I went to the Olympics. That was for sure the single greatest contribution he ever made to my life."

Rowing is a small enough thing that by working at it the athlete can strive to be the best in the world. Because it is so specialized, it is somewhat artificial. Inside its controlled environment, measurement is by one single factor — performance at the World Championships. Everyone in the rowing world is young, fit and beautiful. All emotions are felt with desperate keenness. Joy and disappointment are orchestrated to fit the cycle of wins and losses. The cycle does not allow the complexities of the outside world to intrude. The rowing world is like a glass bowl — it distorts things seen through it.

When the stern realities of life force their way in, the glass bowl can crack and break. Athletes who want to keep the bowl together then must integrate the outer world with the rowing world. Heather confronted the outside world's opinion when she went home after training for the 1980 Olympics. She was bitter about the events of the summer but discovered that her family did not think they were worth worrying about. Instead, they questioned the worth of rowing itself. Her father thought maybe she should quit rowing. "What kind of person is it making you into, if you are becoming so bitter?" he wanted to know. Heather's sensitive older sister, Gloria, had just returned from teaching in India, and another sister, Pauline, was working as a nurse in Africa. "What," they asked her, "was the value of rowing, that you would want to suffer it at all?" Why were Heather and Tina so caught up in it? Heather tried to relate the pleasure she found in rowing to the joy that Gloria found in playing the cello. But Gloria could counter that with the fact that in music she was glorifying God and teaching others.

Heather agonized over the worth of rowing for a long time. She finally decided that, arbitrary as it is, rowing is as real a world as any other. Personally, she could grow within it, test her limits, care about others, just as she could anywhere else. She loves the discipline the rowing regimen imposes on her in realizing her potential. Showing people the possibility of realizing their own dreams is something that helps to make following her dream to the Olympics worthwhile. But, in the final analysis, it's pure physical pleasure, and she has stopped apologizing for that.

Heather says, "It really hit me one day in the spring of 1987 what rowing meant to me. I had had a heavy day at work. When I got home my bike wasn't there, and after looking for it high and low, I decided it had been stolen. I was pacing in front of my building, when my boyfriend, Hardolph, showed up. He walked with me the two miles to the rowing club because by this point I didn't feel like doing my workout. He had just finished his and was willing to row a second time to encourage me.

"When I got on the water, it took me about an hour to unwind and make the boat go well. Finally I was really enjoying myself. I was in my brand-new Swiss-made Staempfli single, which I had worked all year to pay for. When we docked, a guy in his forties was flirting from the other dock with some teenage girls. 'I'm coming to get you,' he called to them. I thought they were all crazy swimming in that icy water. He dived in and swam towards the girls on my dock. I thought, 'He's swimming towards my boat! He's not going around it. He's reaching up

onto my boat...he's climbing into my boat!'... 'Get off my boat!'
I screamed. No response. He hoisted his weight onto the fragile
splashboard. I had an oar in my hand. I pushed the spoon of the
oar into his face. 'Get OFF my boat! You'll break it!' Then I
saw the blood trickling down his cheek. My friend intervened
and said in an authoritative voice, 'Look here, this boat costs
$7,000. It is very fragile and it can't be easily replaced.' The
guy, unhurt, said quite casually, 'Oh, sorry about that,' and
moved. I started apologizing profusely, and tried to explain that
I didn't mean to hurt him but didn't know any other way to get
him to respond quickly enough. I figured that my boat would
have been wrecked before he got the message.

"Shaking, I carried my single up into the boat bay. I had
resorted to physical measures to protect my boat. I didn't think
I could do something like that. Hardolph said I shouldn't feel so
badly about it — that the guy was obviously a bit drunk. But it
bothered me that he didn't react more to my behaviour. I
wondered if he was used to being treated like that. I ran home
from the club and kept reliving my reaction. It came to me that
my boat really meant an awful lot to me. It wasn't materialism
at all. My boat represented my freedom, everything I loved about
rowing. Because of all the negative things that have happened
to me in rowing, I need to get back to my bottom line. Even if
at some point I can't compete at the Worlds or Olympics, I know
I always have rowing. And I need to know that. No one can take
away from me that I love to row. I love the power of sending my
boat singing through the water."

The value of sport to the athlete is that it allows her to achieve
transcendence by focusing her consciousness in physical effort.
Competing against others can help push the athlete to that highest
level. As a concert is a celebration for the musician, so is the
race performance for the athlete. It is a way to celebrate her gifts.
It is a privilege to have that opportunity, although every person
ought to have it as a right. The political part is fighting for the
chance to get to the competition, but the pleasure is something
to create anywhere.

5

NO GUTS, NO GLORY

The national team is the big apple of the rowing world. The goal of being on it is dangled in front of rowers' eyes pretty well from the time they first pick up an oar, if they are the right size. For women the "right size" is anywhere from a stocky and mesomorphic five feet nine inches to a lean or heavy six feet four. Beyond a generic big and strong, there is no one body type for the international oarswoman. Success in rowing depends on a certain base level of natural talent, but given that, it depends a lot more on the athlete's persistence, drive, dedication and mastery of the skill of rowing. While many rowers have athletic backgrounds in other sports, many others find in rowing a sport where they can excel in a big way for the first time. And they are thrilled to be doing it.

Rowers are motivated to try out for and then to stay on the national team because they love rowing. But their attachment has many different faces. The desire to excel. The comfort of belonging to the team group. The addictive thrill of racing. One varsity athlete admitted lusting after the status symbol of black tights when she saw some national team women come into the boathouse wearing black tights. "Everyone knew that black tights meant national team, because at that time you could only get them in Europe." But in the long run, the activity of rowing itself and the challenge of being the best in the world is what keeps people in. As Jane Tregunno puts it, "Everyone talks about doing it for their country and wearing the Canada jacket. Maybe that gets you through parts of the Olympic year, but you have to like the day to day and feel inspired all those times you're by yourself, too." Rowing is training, is being tough when tired, is putting up with a lot of crap. Athletes have to love that training for its own sake.

"Hey, they ought to add another test to physiological testing," jokes Rudy. "You don't just improve your oxygen uptake or your strength. They should measure the number of layers of epidermal tissue you develop. Normal people have nine, and rowers grow eighteen. My skin now is a good half centimetre thicker than it was before I started coaching. You know what I mean?"

The oarswomen competing on the 1988 Olympic team know what he means. They grew thick skins on their climb up the international rowing ladder. The toughening process, mental and physical, began years ago.

"In 1981, when I was the team spare," remembers Tina, "I ate and ate to keep my weight up. I would get on the scales and it would say 139. Every morning we cycled six miles to do weights and then back five miles to the course to row twenty-four kilometres. That was straight, no food. No wonder I was losing weight.

"One morning during weights Rudy said we were going to do a weigh-in. And I thought, 'If he finds out I weigh 139, he'll never put me in the boat.' I was racing against another girl all summer for a seat in the four. I was really worried about that weigh-in. And then I thought, 'Aha! I'll stop at the donut shop.' There was one on the way down. So I stopped and ordered coffee, water, donuts, any liquid that I could find. And then I got back on my bike. I could barely cycle. When I got to the boathouse I said to Heather, 'Tell me when they get to the last couple of people for weighing.' And I stood by the water fountain like people did in high school when they made their underweight coxswain drink and drink water before the weigh-in. And that's what I did. Drank and drank. And I went and weighed in at 148 and Rudy said, 'I'm proud of you for keeping your weight up. That really makes me happy.' And then we had to go out for a two-hour row. I was nearly sick. But I achieved my purpose."

Size for rowers is still really important. The crews that stand on the podium at the World Championships to receive their medals year after year are composed of big women, women who weigh 170 pounds, who are well over five feet ten inches. But a few successful oarswomen are smaller than that. They can make up for their smaller size if they are gifted with strength and good cardio-vascular ability. The way they demonstrate their strength and power is in tests on the rowing ergometer. The ergometer simulates the pulling in the rowing stroke and measures the athlete's power output. Athletes do at least four ergometer tests a year to monitor their physiological improvement. For selection to the Olympic team, they need to improve their absolute scores and also achieve a standard level.

In 1979, after her first summer competing on the national team, Heather started her third year of university, expecting to get carded —to get a living and training allowance and have her tuition paid. In November she learned that she hadn't been recommended for the assistance because she didn't have potential. The magic measure of potential in rowing is size. No potential meant no money, no food. Heather had no savings, as the team had trained too hard for her to hold a job. In desperation she raked leaves. By December she had only pickle juice and vinegar in her refrigerator.

The first rowing ergometer test in Canada took place at Upper Canada College in Toronto on the first weekend in December of 1979. It was an experiment for athletes and selectors, and all the athletes were required to do it. Heather used her last $20 to pay for her trip to Toronto. She stopped eating on Thursday, since the cupboard was bare. On Saturday she took the 5:30 a.m. train to arrive on time, but ended up waiting until 7 p.m. to do the four-minute test. When her turn came, she went into a little room. There was the machine — bright orange — and around it were people holding clipboards, stopwatches and rate-watches. The thrill of water and waves and other boats makes racing an aesthetic experience as well as a war of nerves. For this performance, by contrast, Heather suffered the sensory overload of a laboratory rat.

"I sat down on the sliding seat and tied my feet in the footstops, as I would in a boat," recalls Heather. "I had to pull on a wooden bar, which supposedly replicated the oar. The bar was the crosspiece of a metal bar, six feet long, which was attached to a flywheel. At each stroke that wheel spun with a whining whiz — now the mere thought of the sound makes my heart pound. A counter ticked off the revolutions and laid bare my sins — not enough endurance, inadequate strength, lack of desire. I finished the test, gasping for air, but hardly able to draw breath for the pain of it."

After wrestling with the erg, Heather crept off down a lonely corridor. Upper Canada College was deserted on a Saturday night. She lay face down on the hall floor. She pushed her belly into the tile, and rocked side to side for half an hour in mute pain. A few weeks later she got a phone call saying that she had the top ergometer score among the Canadian oarswomen. Although small, she had proven she had the less obvious physiological gifts of high lactic acid tolerance and an excellent cardiovascular system. As a result, Rowing Canada decided to recommend her to Sport Canada for carding. No more pickle juice.

Rowers usually get carded by performing in the top half of the field at the World Championships. A few, though, receive carding by showing potential — by pulling outstanding ergometers or by being big, although size does not automatically indicate physiological ability. The search is always on for the winners of the next gold medal. Older, established athletes can be ousted from the team by contenders who are beneath them, but close enough to promise physiological superiority by the time of the Olympics.

In 1988, from March on, the rowers' schedule is full with training for the Olympics. They work out twice a day. It usually takes half an hour to get to the training site at Elk Lake. Upon arrival they stretch out for half an hour. Then they go out to row anywhere from twelve to twenty-four kilometres, which takes from seventy minutes to two hours. In the early part of the season they row the longer distances at a steady stroke rating, to build up their general fitness level and to get used to rowing with each other. As the races get closer, the practices become shorter, sharper and more intense. Rowers will do repetitions of high-rate pieces one to five minutes long, for a total of twenty to forty minutes of hard pulling, depending on the type of work. After getting off the water, they discuss the session, occasionally watch videos of the practice, stretch out, then return home.

During the periods when they train full time, rowers go home after practice to eat, then shower and sleep. Their training and competitive schedules make it difficult for them to hold jobs, although most do for part of the year. They are more likely to fit in employment or school during the winter months, when training isn't so time-consuming and there isn't any international competition. During the two waking hours between practices when they are rowing full time, though, rowers may get physio treatment, do laundry or go grocery shopping. Then at 4 p.m. or so it's off to practice again. Around 7 p.m. they go home for the evening to eat, veg out and sleep.

Through the year the cycle and type of training vary. Athletes peak for the World Championships at the end of the summer by rowing intensively for at least the five months leading up to them. In the summer they live and train together in Victoria or Vancouver, B.C., London or St. Catharines, Ontario, depending on where their coach lives. They compete as the Canadian team in two to three international races over the summer before the Worlds. In the fall the athletes return to their own home cities. For two weeks in September they take a break. Because the 1988 Olympics are being held in late September, the athletes' break will come in October. Then through the fall they train nine or ten times a week — two or three hours a day. The less intensive period helps the rowers to recover from the peak of the World

Championships. During the fall season they race about five times, usually in club or university crews.

The fall races are longer and less intense than the summer races. Called "head races," the fall races are four to five kilometres long, over winding river courses instead of on the straight marked six lanes of summer racecourses. Boats start ten or so seconds apart and try to pass each other. The crown of the fall season is the Head of the Charles Regatta in Boston in mid-October. The biggest single-day regatta in the world, the Charles is the equivalent of homecoming football for rowers — they get back together with far-flung friends for the weekend.

Athletes often forgo the luxury of boating off docks at head races. Often, the boat trailors park where they can get access along the shore. The crews walk into the water with their boats, their footless black tights rolled up to their knees. Unlike in summer races, crews do a running start so that the boat is moving at full speed well before the starting line. The athletes get the thrill of a new shot of adrenalin each time they pass a slower crew ahead of them.

After racing, crews make their leisurely way back down the course, stopping frequently in the crush of boats. They find out who won by inspecting computer time sheets on shore. Or else someone might come running with the news. Then, forgetting the glass and rocks underfoot, they march beaming onto the shore. And discover the cuts later when — the euphoria dimmed — they put on socks and shoes.

In the winter, athletes do a high volume of training, ten to twelve workouts a week, two to three hours a day. They do three two-hour weight-training sessions a week to build their strength — power cleans with Olympic bars and free weights at anywhere from 135 to 175 pounds, leg press in the 300- to 500-pound range and squats, bench pulls, bench press. Starting into heavy weights means being so stiff it hurts to ease oneself down on a toilet seat for the first week. Rowers do two or three cardiovascular workouts to build their fitness level — in snowbound parts of Canada that means fifty to ninety minutes of running, cross-country skiing or ergometer rowing with a target heart-rate of 150 to 170 beats a minute. What Canadian rowers lose in time on the water during the winter, they perhaps gain in not getting stale. In the third type of training, rowers do two or three "MVO2" workouts a week to increase their power and intensity for the seven-minute summer racing distance. (MVO2 stands for maximum volume of oxygen — these workouts measure in litres the oxygen that muscles take from the blood for energy.) A usual MVO2 workout is ten hard three-minute pieces on an ergometer, with equal recovery time — just light rowing — in between. The winter training regimen prepares rowers for the intensity of the spring and summer seasons.

All year, but especially during the summer months, the athletes' eating and sleeping patterns and body weight are check-ed. They consume 4,000 to 7,000 calories a day. Of those calories, 65 per cent are complex carbohydrates — grains, legumes, fruit and vegetables — which supply basic energy and help depleted muscles restore themselves. The balance of the diet should be some 25 per cent fats and 10-12 per cent protein. On the whole, they stay away from junk food and alcohol. Canadian rowers do not take performance-enhancing drugs like steroids. Rowers frown on steroids, but perhaps they can get away with not taking them because rowing is such a low-profile sport that they have no financial incentives to do so. There is no professional circuit to move on to after retirement from the na-tional team, and there are no big juicy endorsements for top per-formers to snag. Athletes take their heart-rates each night and morning on waking. They record their moods, for mood indi-cates stress levels and fatigue. But despite all their care, athletes can still wear themselves out.

"The doctor says I'm overtrained," said Lisa in December 1987. "It's really frustrating because for four weeks I'm only al-lowed to train at under a 120 heart-rate. I'm afraid I'll get be-hind." Heart-rates during training should range from 150 to 195 beats a minute, depending on the type of workout. Lisa's rest-ing heart-rate is 47 when she is healthy. "I didn't know I could be overtrained given the sort of intensity we've been training at, but the doctor said it has nothing to do with intensity, but rather enough recovery time in between workouts. Drew says it's highly unlikely I'm overtrained, as I haven't exhibited any of the psychological symptoms. So I guess I'd better start weeping all the time and complaining and dragging myself around."

While volume is still important, intense training, broken by periods of rest to recover, leads to physiological improvement. But the training orthodoxy used to be that more was always better. Training is much more scientific now than even a few years ago.

"We rowed over twenty kilometres two times a day for the seven days we were at our spring training camp one year," says Jane Tregunno. "We ran down to the boathouse from the hotel, although we usually got a ride back. No one had calloused hands anymore because of the winter break from rowing, so everyone got terrible blisters. I got blood poisoning on my hand from the river water infecting my open blisters. We got blisters on our bottoms from the seats. In between workouts we would crawl to the dining room at the University of Pennsylvania, and then crawl to our beds at our hotel and pass out with exhaustion."

Their hands seem to be permanently calloused now. Labourers from the Old Country shake their heads and cluck their tongues when they see the thick pads of skin that have built up at the roots of the oarswomen's fingers. These women of the New World are used to working hard, but now they are not interested in being tough just for the sake of being tough. That's macho behaviour, and they don't need it. Some of them, though, still feel guilty, thinking maybe they aren't as tough as they should be.

"I feel like a wimp when I decide not to row when the lake looks rough," says Barb Armbrust, who trains at Elk Lake. "On windy days in the winter I'm kind of afraid I might tip. I don't feel all that confident in my single. I almost always go out, though." She has won several international sweep medals in her nine years of rowing and has been sculling in Victoria for about two years. She is right to be worried. One weekend in January 1988, two novice men's eights from the University of Victoria were swamped by icy waves during a sudden squall. The sole coach there fished the nine athletes from one of the crews out of the water and loaded them all into her launch. But the overladen launch floundered a hundred metres from shore. By the time they swam in and got help, the nine athletes in the other crew had been in the water for forty-five minutes. One athlete was not found. Eight rowers were taken to hospital to be treated for hypothermia. One of them died soon after arrival. Even though on that occasion no one could have foreseen the abrupt change in the weather, when tragedy strikes, the athletes must rethink what's machismo and what's necessary in pre-Olympic winter training.

The time of greatest stress is the drama of final spring selection. In 1988 the drama lasts for months. Round One is the March selection camp. Round Two is the May Speed Order Race. Round Three is the battle for a finish in the top half of the field at the Lucerne Rotsee Regatta in July. Round Four is the last resort — some crews may have the option of racing a time standard against the clock at the Olympic Basin in Montreal in August.

In Round Two, the May Speed Order, the sweep rowers demonstrate their finesse in pairs, the smallest and most sensitive sweep boat. Scullers row in their singles. The winners may choose to be the national team pair or single. The other top finishers are then invited to seat-race for other crews. In seat-racing, the coaches race different combinations of athletes against each other in two crews. After one 2,000-metre race, athletes are switched from one crew into the other. They race again. The race times are tallied up over a number of races and show up which athletes have the fastest times consistently. These athletes are selected to the crew. Seat-racing is nervewracking because athletes never know when they will be switched and they always feel that their own neck is on the line.

As well as seat-racing, there are subjective components in selection.

"Sport is such a competitive venue," says Rudy Wieler. "What we try to do, to get along with each other, is create rules. The problem is, rules deal with human beings. The athletes fought very hard for rules in selection and everything, but in some ways that may have hurt them. It takes away from the flexibility that a coach may have had....The gut feelings, intangibles, are very important. Sure we've got to quantify everything, but there are qualitative components as well." In 1988 the selection procedures are written down to protect the athletes from arbitrary decisions, although there is still room for some subjectivity.

Athletes know that qualitative components are an essential part of selection, but on occasion they have had difficulty trusting the gut feelings of the coaches. They have seen times when the coaches' gut feelings were based on something as inconsequential as an athlete's facial expression. One coach didn't trust Lisa to pull hard, because she didn't grimace when she rowed.

Even golden girls have their bad moments, as Jane discovered when she almost lost her "A" card for trying to buck the system ("A" cards receive $650 a month and keep the card for two years). She learned the limits of athletes setting their own course when she tried to select which boat she would row in 1985. When she said that she would not compete for a seat in the quad, since she wanted to row the double, Jane and her chosen partner, Lisa Wright, were told that it was the quad or nothing. Jane and Lisa, also a 1988 Olympic contender, then challenged to row the pair. The pair, unlike the double, was open to challenge — that is, whoever won the trials could be the national team boat. Jane and Lisa fulfilled selection requirements, and therefore carding requirements, by racing the pair. When they lost the trials, however, they not only missed the World Championships, they almost lost their carding. Their carding should not have been questioned, for they trained and competed for the pair according to the selection rules. It was their earlier noncompliance over the matter of the double and the quad that was held against them.

"I was only aware of being the golden girl," says Jane, "when in the later years it wasn't like that. I looked back and realized how lucky I had been. I saw again the bad things that happened to other people. Eventually your time comes when something happens to you, and you realize how good it was before."

Although coaches and other members of the selection committee may or may not have personal favourites, "coachability" is used as a selection factor when two athletes are otherwise evenly matched. Getting along well with everybody doesn't matter a bean if the person cannot move a boat. However, if an athlete is seen as difficult, such a reputation can negatively influence the selection committee. Thus, in selection, athletes want to ensure that only one outcome is possible — that they outperform their fellow competitors.

"Right now I think the best situation you can get yourself in is winning the Speed Order in the pair or the single and then being master of your own fate," states Lisa. "I don't trust the program to put together the fastest boats. They've done some things right. But I don't feel I can count on them to be consistent."

Lisa's bottom line in 1988 is this: "Athletes need to have more input; they have a lot of good ideas and have their finger on the button. We should be treated with some respect for what we know about rowing. It has happened to some extent but it should happen more." After giving a number of her ideas to her teammates, since she wasn't asked by the director, she adds, tongue-in-cheek, "Boy, I'd make a great HPD-ess, wouldn't I?" (HPD means high performance director — sports administration jargon.)

"Any given year where we have a poor selection process in one element — like we did in 1986 with the women —we have a huge kafuffle," admits Jim Joy. "We try to minimize those distractions because that leaves a bad taste in people's mouths and it hurts their performance."

In 1986, however, it seemed that for all but the top crews, politics, rather than performance, dictated which boats people were in. The four was selected by extensive seat-racing. After that was all over, Heather and Lisa, the last two cuts from the coxed four, were not seat-raced for the pair, the next sweep boat. Instead, they were put in the double sculls without being raced. The reason? Lisa did not want to row for Rudy, who was coaching the pair, so she and Heather got the double as a consolation prize. Neither of them were accomplished scullers. Meanwhile, two athletes whom Heather and Lisa had beaten during the seat-racing for the four were put in the pair because they could work better with Rudy. And to top it all off, several scullers were condemned to rowing sweep in the eight. All the seat-racing and ranking of the athletes had been done in sweep boats, so these scullers never had a chance to prove themselves as scullers.

"Everyone in our eight felt burned because they thought they should have been elsewhere," explains one member of the crew that had the worst time in that summer of 1986. "They were mad at the double because they managed to escape the real punishment of the mistakes that were made. It was a circus at that selection. Everyone got fed up. And the coaches and selectors were power-struggling over these people who were watching their lives drop as one play or another went on between them. They were treating the women as if they were playthings — it was their power, theirs to do what they wanted with. It was just disgraceful. I'd never seen such a fiasco. For those women it just was one more kick in the teeth."

In 1986, when they were sculling in the double, Heather and Lisa decided to focus on the challenge of sculling rather than think about why they should be in the four or the pair, or why the eight thought they should not be the double. They were able to handle the situation because they had been through the mill and knew what getting upset could cost them. Lisa says, "I'm really pleased with how rowing in the double that summer went, how Heather and I prepared ourselves. We really learned a lot from each other, but I also realized that it would take a while to get to the level in sculling that I was in sweep."

In 1984, when she'd been team alternate, Heather had learned what getting upset could cost. She had retired that fall. But as she thought over her rowing career, she gradually changed her mind. In 1985 she went to Switzerland for the summer. In August she went to watch Tina's crew come from behind the Russians to win a bronze medal at the World Championships in Belgium.

After the races, the Canadian athletes traded away all their red and white training gear in the post-race milling about and exchange of goods. Tina and Heather meandered towards the bus to go back to the hotel. Heather told Tina of her conversation with the sculling coach that afternoon. "He walked up to me and said, 'I hear you're planning to try out for the sculling team.' When I said I planned to row, all he said was 'Hmmph!' and then he walked away. I get the feeling that no one could care less. It's discouraging."

Tina stopped walking and looked squarely at her older sister. "So what! Heather, it doesn't matter. I've had to fight for years without encouragement." Heather stared down at the asphalt and scuffed her foot back and forth. "It's nice if you get it, but you've got to do it for yourself because you want it. You can't wait for someone to beg you to come back." Thus ended the sermon. Heather remembered Tina's words and decided it was time she developed some of the self-sufficiency and toughness Tina displayed.

The intonation of disapproval in the sculling coach's voice made Heather realize that she had some confronting to do. "I went to Ian McFarlane, my coach, when I got back to Kingston and told him of my goals in rowing," says Heather.

"I wouldn't have any confidence going out into the general population and saying, 'That person can be a champion,'" says Ian. "But if someone has a reasonably competitive history and makes the leap of trust in me to ask, 'Do you think I can do it?' — that's when a person is probably ready to take a charge at going for it. I've never seen anybody ask that question comfortably. And it's certainly not one to answer casually."

"Ian watched me work hard, and I gained his respect," says Heather. "I asked him what hurdles I had to overcome to reach my goals. I had to be aware of how people viewed me, without internalizing their assessment of me. I still found it hard to hear coaches' negative perceptions of me. In coaching me, though, Ian responded to the Heather he saw, rather than the difficult Heather he had heard about.

"At the beginning of my rowing career I was very confident that I could get what I wanted. But when bad things happened to me, I didn't know how to let go of them. My younger brother was killed while Tina and I were racing in Lucerne, in 1983. The day after we heard about his death, and the day before we left for home, we were out in the eight practising. Our coxswain piped the song through the boat with the words 'Take your passion and make it happen.' We started to cry in the boat, because we felt so out of control of what was happening in our lives. That sense that I had no control stayed with me for the next couple of years.

"In 1986, when I was making my comeback, after the year away from rowing, I worked with a sports psychologist. It sounds simplistic, but I had to identify my bottom line — I could always leave rowing if I didn't like it. It's not much of an option, but at least once I had established that, I could go on. I listed my goals and what I was prepared to do to achieve them. I realized I need not be a victim, that whatever happened I could always control what *I* felt and did. Even the mess-up of rowing in the double was tolerable, because I made sure I got as much profit as I could out of the situation. But still one hopes for optimal situations and not just tolerable ones."

No athlete can afford to go into the 1988 selection worrying that mistakes made in other years will happen again. Thinking that way erodes their determination to put themselves on the line. There's a fine line between preparing yourself for whatever might happen and setting yourself up for failure. Coach Ian Mc-

Farlane observes that "if the situation is not ideal, the athlete's response can be positive or negative. The negative thing is to build little protective devices around you. We've seen lots of people do that. Put so many roadblocks around their career that they just didn't achieve. The positive response is, 'Things can go haywire around me, but I'm not going to move.' You need to believe that the platform you're doing your work on is stable. It's partly faith and it's partly stubbornness, and it's partly a low-grade, constant intensity."

"The summer of 1987 could have been horrible for me," says Tina. "Lisa and I were spares that year. It really hurt my pride to be in a situation where I had no control. All I could do was the best I could. But when I didn't make the four, I thought it was really going to hurt. Lesley kept telling me that it wasn't just Tricia to whom the four's bronze medal successes of the past two years should be attributed, it was me too. Tricia needs support and that was my role. Setting a solid rhythm.

"The most important thing that summer was when Lisa sat me down and said, 'We're spares. And we have to be able to be spares and not let it get to us, because it's important for the team that we're positive. And it's important for our own psyches not to be getting really depressed, because we are good.' Lisa's ability to look at any situation and take the best out of it is amazing. She turned what for me could have been a very difficult situation into something that was really strong by saying, 'This is our role, and how are we going to best perform it?' And besides, we were racing in the eight that was being thrown together. We actually planned it out as if we were in any other crew, racing. Instead of training to race, our training was to not race and deal with that. It was a big job and maybe we were unusual in that we approached it that way."

While women tend to respond to adverse situations by feeling as though they have no control over what happens, the oarswomen who have survived are oriented towards mastering the challenges in front of them. They have gotten hard knocks and picked themselves up again, using the experience to motivate themselves.

Kay says of the struggles, "It's our personalities — all of us thrive with that kind of friction. Athletes taking charge of the situation."

But confidence can't take root unless there is positive reinforcement at some point. Tina early developed an air of confidence in herself. "My seeming confidence must come from having trained in a really supportive and competitive environment at Princeton. A group of us were trying out for national teams, but they were for the American team. I didn't seriously compete for my seat against that core group. They helped push me forward and gave me the confidence that I could do it. I knew I was good. And everyone else at Princeton thought so too." Tina still hadn't proved herself on the national team. "My success in 1983, when I broke through onto the national team, had a lot of factors to it. In 1982 I had a bad year. I'd been sick and had to re-evaluate whether I wanted to row, after I got cut from the national team. The fall of 1982, I had no interest in rowing for a couple of months. I only trained because I hadn't decided not to. Then I decided I'd go for it. I guaranteed I would sleep for eight hours a night and do two practices a day, that I was going to spend every evening in the library until 11 p.m., at which point I'd go home to bed.

"The thing that came out of Woodstock and Doug Clark, too, was that if you did the prescribed program, you knew you had to be better than everybody else. You couldn't believe anyone else was being quite as strict as you were. Also, someone said to me that to really succeed in rowing you had to have a lot of people massaging your ego. That's one thing I had in 1983. At Princeton, in final year, the seniors feel like the world is theirs. I just had an incredible time. I was asked out more times than I had ever been in my life. Everything was falling into place for me, things that I'd waited for. Once I'd gotten my priorities in line I could go after anything I wanted. With that in mind I came to the 1983 Speed Order with a totally different attitude. Every year before I'd come hoping, but this year I came really confident. I'd done my thesis, I'd made lasting friends, I stayed healthy all year."

Talking about the power of positive thinking has been enough to make self-respecting rowers sick. When sports psychologists first started working with the national team in the early 1980s, coaches and athletes alike responded negatively. Men's sweep coach Neil Campbell has stated that any rower who needs to see a psychologist shouldn't be rowing anyway. But many coaches have realized that confidence can be enhanced. Still, rowers and coaches completely mistrust self-deception. Confidence must be based on desire, hard work, and realism.

Angie discovered the importance of the desire for achievement in rowing in 1986. She made the team because she performed adequately by objective measures after having suffered a herniated spinal disc that year. But she found she didn't need to prove anything to herself anymore through racing. She had put her intensity into a personal relationship and her Ph.D. studies, and the ideal of pursuing excellence in the sport context, which had so inspired her in earlier years, now changed its form. She retired from rowing when the summer ended.

"In Nottingham, at the World Championships, I tried to work myself up to race," recalls Angie. "For my mindgames, I painted these blades, the six blades of the countries in our final. And I'd cross them out with black masking tape. I had this thing up on my wall. It had worked for me before, at the Olympics. But this time I just looked at the wall and laughed. Who am I trying to kid? I could care less. At the Worlds, in our lane draw, we had the Soviets on one side and the East Germans on the other. And our coxie was saying, 'Now everybody look across at the person on your left side and the person on your right side. And just think to yourself, I can beat this person.' And I looked at the woman on the left of me and the woman on the right, and laughed. Who am I kidding? She weighs 220 and she weighs 190, and right now I weigh 147. They're going to cream me."

Racing is a mindgame, once the physical preparation of rowing is over. Tina describes their race in the coxed four at the 1985 Worlds.

"Two of us in the crew never medalled before, so convincing ourselves we could win a gold medal was what broke us into the medals. If we'd convinced ourselves we could come second or third, I don't think we would have medalled. In 1985, though, I felt prepared to race the race. Our crew was never something that naturally gelled; the speed was something we worked for. But I knew that we were the kind of crew that could come from behind. During the race there was never any question that we could do it, even though we were in sixth place at the 500-metre mark. It was more of a question of what the steps of a race could be. For all five of us, it was the result of the disciplined mindset we'd trained over the summer. We thought — 'No one's expecting anything from the Canadian women's four, and we're going to have to challenge from behind. Be prepared not to get distracted if there are crews ahead of you. Think of attacking.' Our race plan was really detailed in every 250 metres about how we were going to attack people and move through them. We just executed it.

"But when we were done, Barb, Lisa and I were really dejected. Tricia turned around and said, 'Well, how does it feel? You've finally won a medal.' And I said, 'It feels pretty awful.' And then we got our medals. We'd started doing okay by then. And then we got off the water and said, 'This is silly.' We had an excellent race and that was the best we could do at that point. But because we had to build ourselves up to win a gold medal we were going to come away feeling dejected. In retrospect it was a great race because we taught ourselves to be disciplined and race against all odds. It was a real breakthrough. I think my expectations of myself are very high, so I don't bother myself with other people's expectations."

These athletes are experienced. As they train for Seoul, they know what they're up against. In 1984 Angie was confident for good reason. She and her crew had done the work. "When we talked to reporters during that pre-race time, I said to them I believed we had a chance for the gold. They'd say, 'How are you so sure?' And I was thinking, 'Of course I know. I didn't get here by not knowing, or by feebly reaching around in the dark." The same is true for the women on the 1988 team.

Bra to the rescue: at the Dad Vail Regatta in Philadelphia, May 1981, Angie Schneider rowed to victory in the University of Western Ontario Varsity Women's Eight with Lesley Thompson's bra securing her broken foot-stretcher.

The 1981 Canadian women's rowing team pose for their official photograph at the Henley course in St. Catharines, Ont., August 1981. Back row, left to right: Lesley Thompson, Kay Worthington, Jane Pringle, Jane Tregunno, Andrea Schreiner, Rudy Weiler. Front row, left to right: Vicki Harber, Cathy Lund, Sylvia Wetzl, Heather Clarke.

Team members training in an eight before final crew selection. Elk Lake, Victoria, B.C., March 1984.

Graduates of the 1984 carpools: one-half of the women's eight and Heather Clarke (right) after their Olympic final at Lake Casitas, July 1984. Front, left to right: Tina Clarke, Cathy Lund, Leslie Anderson, Heather Clarke. Back, left to right: Lisa Robertson, Kay Worthington.

The coxed four on the medal podium at Lake Casitas, Los Angeles Olympics, August 1984. Left to right: Marilyn Brain, Angie Schneider, Barb Armbrust, Jane Tregunno, Lesley Thompson.

The town of Rodney, Ont., celebrates Angie's Olympic medal with a parade. August 1984.

Politics mix with sport at a post-Olympic celebration, CNE grounds, Toronto, August 1984.

Kay Worthington (left) and Silken Laumann (right) — pre-race zaniness at the World Championships in Hazewinkel, Belgium, August 1985. Note Silken's Canadian flag tattoo in lipstick.

Prince Philip shakes Tina Clarke's hand after the coxed four's victory in the Commonwealth Games in Edinburgh, July 1986. Left to right: Lesley Thompson, Jane Tregunno, Jenny Walinga, Tricia Smith.

The Canadian men's four on the medal podium at the Commonwealth Games, Edinburgh. Left to right: Grant Main, Paul Steele, Kevin Neufeld, Pat Turner.

Lesley Thompson gets a winning coxswain's traditional reward — dumped into the water — at the Commonwealth Games. Left to right: Tina Clarke, Jenny Walinga, Jane Tregunno, Tricia Smith.

Heather Clarke (bow) and Lisa Robertson (stroke) rowing the women's double at the August 1986 World Championships in Nottingham.

Indulging in an international rowing passion — knitting sweaters. Tina Clarke and some Romanian oarswomen at the World Championships, Nottingham, England.

Going camping at Long Beach, Vancouver Island, on a precious day off, June 1987. Left to right: Jenny Walinga, Heather Clarke, Katie Burke, Jamie Schaeffer, Jane Tregunno, Ray Collier, Darby Berkhout, Kathryn Barr, Kirsten Barnes, Hardolph Wasteneys.

The intensity of concentration: Silken Laumann in her single at the Pan American Games, Indianapolis, July 1987.

The rigours of practice: Elk Lake, Victoria, August 1987. Left to right: Jane Tregunno, Kathryn Barr, Jenny Walinga, Heather Clarke.

6

SOUL AS A CREW

The Canadian women's four were stretching in their tent one morning before practice at the Olympic course at Lake Casitas in California in 1984. The sun shone down over the lake and the desert hills. Rowers were walking around, stretching, going out to row. The British women's four walked by the Canadian tent. One of them dropped her shorts and pulled a moon.

"It was a challenge," recalls Angie. "The Brits were saying, 'We're more cool than you. We live more dangerously,' even though we beat them on the water. Men play games like this all the time, but women don't so much. But it didn't stop there. Later they sent us a message on the computer system saying, 'Food for thought. Meet us in the cafeteria at 7 p.m.' So we're sitting in the cafeteria, which had windows all around it. And the British women got a little guy in a golf cart to drive them around. They were yelling for the Canadian women's four and then they mooned us a second time. They were saying they were gutsier than us.

"We decided to retaliate. Two days later we sent them a message saying, 'The Empire Strikes Back.' Three of us decided we'd go to the movie theatre and pull moons. We practised in front of mirrors and everything. We went to the theatre set up for the athletes in the Olympic village. We were more nervous than at any other time for the whole Olympics. And everyone came in. We were horrified because we realized the British women must have publicized our message. Then Barb stood up and started swinging her arms and said, 'This is what you've all been waiting for.' And we all went running up to the front and did it. And everyone had brought cameras and all the flashes went off. We felt so much unity in that moment. It was actually far riskier than the final. We were far more tense. We suspended all the other rules of society because we would never pull moons. But we kept the crew communion." And, more importantly, they beat the Brits!

Crew members prove their commitment to each other by doing daring deeds. The mooning helped create a folk memory for the 1984 coxed four, even though only three of the women in the crew did it. Risking in play helped cement the bond that had been created on the water. But all five members of the coxed four proved their bond with each other over months of training together.

Crew demands commitment. Crews must develop a collective identity as "us" against "the world." Rowers tend to be a bit fanatical, and they recognize kindred spirits. They bond because they share so much joy and so much pain. They share certain images — dogwood blossoms and traffic jams on the busy Henley course in St. Catharines; the sun rising over the bluffs on London's Fanshawe Lake, which is perfectly positioned to catch the worst of north, west and south winds; the Canada geese at Burnaby Lake near Vancouver. Memories of gliding peacefully through ochre November dawns, the mist rising off the lake. Getting drenched from head to toe by waves on windy spring afternoons. Cursing coach-boat swells. The quick rise of the word "fuck" to the lips when windsurfers get in the way of the boat. Hating the coach. Griping about the coxswain. Thinking you should stroke the boat until you're put in the stroke seat. Wishing the person in front of you would row properly so the boat would run perfectly.

Grumbling about having to go out to the lake. Hoping that a surprise thunderstorm will cancel morning practice so you can sleep in. Grumbling when weather conditions mean you cannot row. Driving to a donut house for donuts and coffee (not too often). Standing in huddles at the boathouse, catching up on scandals, on the latest rowing romance, instead of stretching. Lifting weights in dingy, dank rooms. Running in snowstorms. Filling in logbooks two weeks late. Ergometer tests. Lactic acid tolerance workouts. Twelve-hour road trips through the night to regattas. Being screwed up once again by the hurry-up-and-wait mentality. Knitting endless Icelandic sweaters at regattas to while away the time before the race. Hugs. Massages. Blisters. Stiff, sore muscles. Aching lower backs. Lycra. Body awareness. Cheesecake pigouts. Quick assessment of a competitor's height, weight, mental toughness. Rowing tans on the front of the knees, backs of shoulders. Dancing all night to the Rolling Stones, with the sweat flying. Falling asleep everywhere. Unopened textbooks. Part-time jobs. Waiting for carding cheques. Housing stray rowers on foam mattresses in the living room. Getting your money's worth at all-you-can-eat buffets.

Racing. The eight becomes one. Bonds cement.

One athlete remembers racing for the University of Western Ontario crew, full of national team members and hopefuls, against a stronger crew from the University of Victoria. The race was a special one, dubbed "Road to the Olympics" and held in Vancouver a week after the regular varsity season ended in November 1982. Daylight Savings Time had ended, so the night drew down at 5:30. The Fanshawe Dam had been let out to lower the lake level for the winter. Alone, the women honed their race to its finest. Person for person they knew that UVic was better than they were. But the Western crew thought they had more soul as a crew.

The two crews started their race at the 1,000-metre mark on the 2,000-metre marked course. The day had been dark and cloudy, but suddenly the sun appeared over snowcapped Mount Baker and shone down. At the "P— " of "Partez!," the starting command, dignified Lesley leaned forward and shrieked "Go!" The Western boat jumped forward. Lesley talked to them, low and intense, guiding them through the race. "Come on, I've got their stroke seat... Now I'm even with seven. I want six. Good, good ... Give it to me. I want five seat, I want their four." None of the crew remember any pain, anything at all from that race except the sheer joy of the power and the awareness that it was perfect. And that they drew ahead with every stroke. When they eased it down, they all cheered: "We beat them, we beat them!" Nothing modest or self-effacing about that victory. And although they were exhausted, they went down across the border to a scummy bar and danced the night away. For all the women in that crew, four of whom would be Olympians in 1984, that was one of the best races they had ever experienced.

With all the camaraderie coexists the contradiction. Competition against teammates. Fundamental detachment. Ruthlessness. Survival.

In the free-fall of training and testing, before the crews are chosen, partnerships form and disintegrate with bewildering rapidity. The pecking order changes with every selection, so there is always tension. It minimizes once crews form.

Tension runs the highest between athletes who row on the same side, port or starboard. "In 1984 everyone I was close to rowed port," says Angie, who rowed starboard. "I don't know if that was subconscious, but I don't know what I would have done if I'd had to compete for a seat in the four against Kay, who rowed portside, lived with me and who I thought would make the crew. And with Heather, I was really torn about her. She taught me how to train well and obsessively. I knew she wasn't going very well that spring. She came up to me once after a video session and said, 'You're rowing really well.' She had been in the coach boat because she had tendinitis and a back injury. I said, 'Thank you. But you've got to calm down.' No one wanted to row with Heather because she was getting anxious and making them anxious. I knew her from Western, that she was wonderful and strong and patient — as patient as you ever are in a crew. She was good, when she relaxed. When she wasn't, the difference was amazing. I felt I owed her, because she'd helped and supported me. But I didn't know how to change things. I think when it ended up being a fight between Tina and her for a seat in the eight that it got to be the worst."

Tina and Heather live the contradiction that is competitive bonding. It wasn't confined to the 1984 selection. "At the May selection in 1986 I really felt like quitting," says Heather. "After ten days of racing and not reaching my goal of making the coxed four, I was exhausted and miserable. I was so disappointed that Tina had made the four and I hadn't. Both of us felt such conflicting emotions. Earlier, she had thought she was going to be cut, and so didn't want to talk to me. When it turned out I was cut from the crew, Tina found me crying behind the boathouse. It was she who encouraged me to keep on going."

In 1987 Heather made the four and Tina didn't. When they were still racing, Heather said to Lisa, "It's awful to have to compete against your sister." Lisa, an only child, returned with the comment, "Heather, we're all family now. We all feel for each other."

It's easier to be ruthless when the enemy is faceless than when the competitors are friends and family. Making the team means beating others. Going to the Olympics means beating others. The athlete must stand alone when she goes for the team. If she cannot take it, she shouldn't be there. Many oarswomen confronted competition for the first time in rowing. They accept the ruthlessness but still empathize with the losers' suffering.

"When I first made the team," says Angie, "the girl I beat out said to me, 'You know when you watch the "Wide World of Sports" introduction, and they show you all the scenes of sports, and they've got the thrill of victory, and then they show a skier falling down the slope, sliding everywhere, smashing and bruising himself — the agony of defeat, that's how I feel.' And I looked at her and said, 'I know.' And I had been the one who defeated her. I didn't care, because thank God it wasn't me. But at the same time, I respected that she was going down that hill. That's what warfare does to you. You build in this defensive mechanism that desensitizes you, but you're incredibly aware."

Men are more used to the contradictions of team bonding than women are. They are brought up with it and usually continue that pattern of friendship throughout their lives. "A rapport continues between a bunch of guys outside the sport environment," says Doug Clark. "It's very strong. Rowing is a way of life among the men. And apart from rowing, they have so many different opportunities to bond on that competitive level. Groups of men will get together, whereas women will get together with one very good friend. But that strong rapport — a sorority — will develop among women rowers over time."

Men learned to compete in Little League Hockey. Women do not traditionally bond on a competitive level because they do not engage in sport as much as men do. Women are also not taught to be as objective about success, failure or criticism as men are.

"Men separate their feelings from their rowing better than women do, although with experience women develop a professional attitude," notes Angie. "For better or for worse, men are trained to feel less sensitive about personal things. In 1984 Neil would scream at Kevin. We could hear him — 'Late! Late! Late! Goddamn it, Kevin, you're late!' — all the way down the course. I would have cringed — 'Everyone in St. Catharines thinks I'm a terrible rower.' But Kevin didn't take it personally. He knew Neil liked him. He didn't have to worry."

Over time, women athletes learn to be objective about personal things. Being objective is a necessary skill, for taking things too personally can hurt a crew by preventing solidarity. But being personal can also work to advantage. Women's crews are more likely to talk out the issues that are bothering them. By talking, they build mutual understanding, mutual trust. They become one another's support system.

"I think I'm more of a loner than a crew person, which is why I like the single," says Andrea Schreiner. "But I've really enjoyed in 1985, 6 and 7 getting to know the other women when I rowed in crews. I survived less-than-perfect coaching situations because the group I was training with got together. And this year, when I was going through the break-up of my marriage, friends came out of the woodwork that I never even knew were there."

Rowers often make friends for life among their teammates. But the bond that develops between them has its genesis in the objective measure of performance. Rowers are on the team to be as fast as they can be. Building mutual trust helps people pull together — pull *for* one another in the boat. When they pull together, they go faster. Therefore, crews consciously work to build the necessary bonds.

A good coach is good because he or she helps to pull the crew together as a unit. Bonding around the coach is the usual pattern for a crew, but the Canadian women's eight discovered that they could bond on their own in 1983. That year, they felt their coach did not give them sufficient direction, so they picked up the slack themselves shortly before the World Championships in Duisberg, West Germany.

"We held a crew meeting to make our own race plan a few days before our final," says Tina. "Our coach, Gil, said, 'Do a start and five strokes, and then just row.'

"Gil operated on the K.I.S.S. principle — 'Keep it simple, stupid.' We felt that we needed a detailed race plan. How can you pull together if you don't know in advance what you're going to do in every stroke? Then we realized pulling together required an attitude of understanding and respect as well as a race strategy.

"We learned a thing or two about group dynamics. All eight of us came from different backgrounds. The four vocal ones, we called ourselves the 'lead girls' because we all fought so hard for control. The lead girls all wanted centre stage and would speak on top of each other, so whoever had the loudest voice got heard. But we grew to appreciate that we should give room for all eight of us to speak."

"The lead girls were really Kay, Tina, Angie and I," says Heather. "We discovered ourselves one day when we really got hyped up after a meeting with the oarswomen from the other countries. During lunch, we discussed women's issues related to rowing, but we had to endure the cynical comments of a few of the men. So as soon as we could, the four of us escaped into our room for a tête-à-tête. It was totally exhilarating — at an allegro pace, staccato style, with wild crescendos. We were leaping up on the bed, interrupting each other and completing each other's sentences. It was a passionate discussion about the meaning of life in the context of rowing. A bit much, eh?

"I didn't want it to end. All the while I was feeling guilty because my friend's repechage race [a second chance at qualifying after an initial heat] was in a few hours. It was his first year at the Worlds, so it was the biggest race of his life so far — it meant qualifying for the finals. He was expecting me to come to his room, as we had agreed, but I couldn't bear to be left out of this wonderful exchange of ideas.

"When all eight of us were there for the crew meetings, the pace changed. We went around the circle to give everyone a chance to speak. We showed each other that everyone's ideas were respected. If a lead girl spoke too long she would get cut off.

"In the end we actually did thrash out a consensus and we raced well. Despite our personality differences, we bonded. But it was funny how different we were. Marilyn Campbell would repeat everything to make sure we all understood. Sarah Ogilvie didn't care what we did as long as everyone 'did their best.' At first we misinterpreted that to mean she didn't care whether or not we won. And Lisa, being new, didn't know what she could contribute. As for me," says Heather, "I can't bear to be left out of anything. I have a tendency to interrupt, and Cathy Lund had trouble getting a word in edgewise."

"I didn't always enjoy the sharp conversations," says gentle Cathy Lund. She retired in 1987 after nearly a decade on the national team. "But the other side of it was thrilling. This was a keen, dynamic group of people with a lot of energy. I learned that I didn't have to like all aspects of someone to like and enjoy them. We bonded because we had so much in common underneath our personalities. It was such a strong environment. I didn't think I was competitive, because I compared myself to the women in my crew. I surprise myself in normal society because I like to lead."

"I didn't identify well with all the women," says Angie of her first summer on the national team. "But by the end of the summer, with us all rowing in the eight, the lead girls were a family. We developed ourselves. It was us against the world."

The athlete-centred bonding of the 1983 lead-girl eight developed by default. The women wanted more direction than their coach gave them; they were exemplary in that they took the trouble to create a direction for themselves. It's often more of a challenge to pull together the second boat on a team into a unit than the top crew, since the athletes in the second boat are often nursing bruised egos. The eight was the second crew that summer, but they saw each other as equals. They made the effort to develop a crew direction.

Unfortunately, 1983 was only one of several years the national team women found the coaches' leadership lacking in other than the top crews. Because of uneven coaching, these women have become used to interacting closely among themselves. They are accustomed to having a lot of autonomy, although individuals among them are still more or less coach-centred, depending on their past experiences. In 1988 the women want to retain their close bonds with one another without excluding the coach, thereby enjoying the best of both worlds.

Athlete-centred bonding can threaten people who aren't used to it. For instance, the coaches misinterpreted the 1983 lead-girl bonds. Instead of looking at the actual situation, they stereotyped the interaction, assuming that the constant debating among the women meant that they weren't getting along .

"Women are more catty than men," says one oarsman. "When something happens in a women's eight on the water, when someone says something they didn't really mean, it's carried onto the land. I've seen that. The same kind of thing goes on in a men's boat, and there's friction, but it's left on the water. The men try to put their personal feelings aside." The coaches in 1983 thought the consensus-building arguments were bitchy, catty. They failed to see the respect and trust that the eight women had developed for one another. The coaches assumed instead that the women, being female, let their personal feelings dictate how they bonded.

Thus, the 1984 selection was set up to include the subjective factors of personality, although the crews were still selected by seat-racing. Selecting crews subjectively is not unknown, but some coaches get away with it better than others do. "Neil likes it when people get along," said a member of his eight. "He's always looking for ways to make the crew go faster and feels that helps, within reason."

"The trust our team had developed began to go sour in the spring of 1984," remembers Tina. "The coaches wanted an insider's view on how we got along, thinking that they could select better crews on that basis. It seemed to us that they tried to convince the coxies that the way to get selected for the team was to be coaches' helpers, not athletes' helpers." Because of their power in helping determine a crew, coxswains walk a fine line between coach and crew. Most of the time, coach, crew and coxswains work together, but during selection time the coxswains can find themselves caught in the middle.

"Rudy had little meetings with us where he made us rank everyone on the team from best to worst and explain why we did it. And then he used it as 'Your teammates think this.' It seemed to me that the ranking came down to really petty things. And that's when people started to feel, 'Oh, maybe we can't trust people as much as we thought we could.'

"Rudy was shocked at my ranking of some of the athletes," continues Tina, "and said, 'Why don't you think she's any good?' I said, 'I don't think she's not any good, I just think that's where she lies.' And he said, 'Why, why, why do you think that?' And I said, 'I refuse to give you any information that is backstabbing to someone on my team, because I don't think that's my job.' He tried and tried to get me to say something, and I refused. He said, 'Well, you know what people say about you, they don't like your sense of humour.' And I thought, 'What's my sense of humour got to do with this? I'm trying out for the team.'"

Angie made Rudy's top crew that year. The previous fall Rudy had said, "When the cream rises to the top, you'll be part of it." And she thought, "I'll be there, even if I have to give up everything to get it." From defining herself as a rebel, she now decided to play ball with the system.

"The coaches always look for a story," she says. "It'll be told anyway, and you might as well tell your side. I thought, 'I'll put it all in the open.' But in our opinion Rudy played mental games to get what he thought was the best performance out of each athlete. Was it fair? I guess it depends whether we're talking about expediency or morality. If we're talking about expediency, if pragmatism is your morality, then what works, works. But if your morality is based on universals, that what is right is right, regardless of the effects, then what Rudy did was wrong. I'm telling you, at that point in time, it was really hard to distinguish anymore. People were telling all these stories, and if you tell them long enough you'll start to believe them, although they just weren't true. I felt there was a slippery slope we were all going down."

The methods used in 1984 reinforced the theory that women are catty. All the women thought it was unacceptable — setting teammates against one another by making them rank each other does not make a strong team. If they do it right, however, coaches can play up competition between athletes and motivate them to put out that extra bit of effort. Such competition is desirable.

"In 1982 when Rudy and I didn't get along, he said I was like a German shepherd," says Angie. "He compared me to another starboard athlete and said she was like a fox terrier that has a hold of your pantleg. She was little and her bite didn't hurt, but she was tenacious. Tenacity was going to win. Rudy questioned whether I had the endurance to beat her. He'd cheer her on and put me up as the 'boo hiss' person."

How the athletes take the competition depends on their relationship with the coach and their relationships with each other. In some situations, the competition bond lays the foundation of a strong friendship.

"In the fall of my freshman year at Princeton University," says Tina, "it became really obvious that our coach, Kris Korzeniowski, was pitting me against Anne Strayer. Strayer is on the American sculling team. Kris noticed a little spark in both of us that was blind with training, training crazy. He wanted to see what he could do to make us motivate each other to better success.

"Strayer pulled me aside one day just before Christmas and said, 'I like you.' I said, 'That's good.' She said, 'Something's going to happen. Kris has taken a look at the two of us. Have you noticed how he puts us on opposing teams for runs and weight circuits? We're always in direct competition with each other. I just want you to recognize this now, so it doesn't hurt our friendship. I think we can learn a lot from each other. Kris can screw us up. He'll try to — he thinks it's amusing.' From then on we knew we must be somewhat similar, or he would never have chosen us. Strayer and I were always trying to show off to each other. She was, in a crazy way, my female role model."

Tina respected Kris. "He was never on the kind of power trip that was threatening to us; he never directed it at his athletes personally. Kris's temper even contributed to our bonding. He's European, so he's allowed to be volatile. Kris used to kick us off the water and say, 'You're pathetic. You row like a *sheeet*. You might as well not row,' and send us home. And we'd stay out there and do pieces, and he'd say, 'I said, go home!' And we'd keep on rowing. And he'd take off and slam his boat up on the dock, and that'd be the end of Kris. And we'd finish our workout."

The crew bonding around the coach is the traditional model for teams. It works when the unit is coach and crew together, although the crew unit is paramount. The athletes are, after all, the ones pulling on the oars.

Neil Campbell's eight in 1984 is the quintessential example of coach-centred bonding that worked. Neil gave the crew the right mix of leadership and free rein to maximize its performance. He demanded conformity — for example, all the guys had to be cleanshaven and they had to spend their days off playing golf together, even if they hated golf. But he also let the crew matrix work itself out.

"There are always one or two people in a crew that stand out as being arrogant," says Olympic medallist Doug Hamilton. "And they always turn out to be the crew motivators. In the eight it is Mike and Mark Evans, in the quad it's me. The rest of the crew bonds around that. Without it, there's something missing. He's the guy that will say in the middle of a piece, 'Look, you guys, you're not working. Get your asses in gear.' Neil Campbell calls it the 'ass-hole factor.' It's hard for the coach to do that because he hasn't got the same respect from the other guys in the crew for being tired too."

"Neil is more than coach," says Kevin. "He's like a friend to us, and that makes a big difference. He emphasizes that." Many of the women simultaneously suspect and envy such solidarity. They are suspicious of what they see as conformity in the coach orientation, and they envy the trust and success. "Neil picks the people he thinks have what it takes. He has an inner circle, an elite to his oarsmen," says one of Neil's former oarsmen. The women would not let their coaches get away with what they see as excessive subjectivity. They feel they've been burned by it.

Still, some of the women hoped that all their problems would end if they got their own Neil Campbell. In November of 1985 Doug Clark came out to the camp in Victoria and was greeted joyfully. Like Neil, Doug has a history of bonding with his athletes, and he also developed some of the athletes currently on the national team. He was appointed head coach of the women's team in 1986.

But too much mistrust had made the women wary — and more self-sufficient. They guarded themselves against the close bond that Doug was used to building on. Their wariness was compounded by the 1986 sweep/sculling selection fiasco. And Doug's frustration was compounded by the lack of support he got from the rowing administration. He arrived at the newly formed training centre to discover that many of the promised funds were not available. He had no motorboat from which to coach his crews. He was given sweep oarswomen whom he had to teach how to scull in only a few short weeks. The good equipment was forgotten somewhere by an administrator, so the athletes had to row in inferior boats. Then, at the Worlds, two of the crew had such bad injuries that they couldn't race their final. On top of that, as Silken says, "We set ourselves up for the fall by looking to Doug Clark as our Neil Campbell." Not surprisingly, the general team trust in a coach that comes from winning was not established. The experience reinforced the women's attitude of independence.

"Winning isn't everything, it's the only thing," goes the saying hanging on Kevin's wall. Kevin modifies it: "Winning helps. Winning made us realize how important the rowing bond was. Before 1984 I had a pretty businesslike approach to rowing. As long as they do their job and I do mine, and we go fast, it's great. We don't have to go out for milkshakes after the row. In 1984 I slowly changed that. I started clueing in that there's more to rowing, that there's friendships. The guys I went through that with, at least the core — you know, if they weren't rowing, I wouldn't either. The week we spent training in Syracuse, New York, a few weeks before the '84 Olympics, was the turning point for that crew. We were just together, ten guys. All we did was row and hack around. And nobody had anything to worry about. The bonds sort of grew together. We went through some pretty tough workouts and were consistent."

"Over time, the athletes and the coach feel each other out and reach an agreement based on ability," says Doug Hamilton. "Knowledge builds respect, on both sides. Trust evolves through a couple of racing seasons, World Championships, high-pressure situations. It's hard to achieve a crew sense of consistency and speed unless you come together year after year."

The older women on the 1988 Olympic team have rowed with each other in many different combinations. They know each other, have built respect. Teammates deal with their differences by making a joke of them. "Because both parties are aggressive," notes Tina, "a rift could easily become a major blowout, since neither person is likely to back down. Having a sense of humour is essential. It's a way of confronting differences indirectly. No one can tell someone directly to do something without getting a negative reaction." The women tease each other about everything from boyfriends to shoe size. They learn to respect the vagaries of personal style by sounding out the desire to win beneath. They prod each other into proving they are serious about racing. They keep clear the goal of the crew.

The intensity of the atmosphere always climbs higher as racing time nears. Nerves start to fray. The athletes are used to the tension because they train towards the goal of the World Championships from May to September every summer. But in Olympic years they spend even more time together, and the stakes are higher. For the 1988 Olympics, the athletes are training together from March until September — seven months.

"The shift from rowing being a part-time activity to controlling our whole lives is hard," says Tina. "You can be really cohesive for the summer and put together a group, but you want to be able to withdraw again and regain a sense of yourself."

Rowers let off steam by partying, though rarely, since they usually have to save themselves for next morning's practice. But their parties' infrequency and corresponding wildness cause them to enter the folk memory of the rowing circuit. "In 1983," remembers Tina, "twenty-two of us stayed in Boston after the Head of the Charles Regatta, both men and women. We were really happy because we all won, and we partied our brains out. We had so much fun together that we made a name for ourselves. When we pulled up at the party in Boston, everyone said, 'The Canadians are coming, the Canadians are here!' And twenty-two of us piled out of the van and everybody went, 'Oh my God!' We still talk about that."

Tina continues: "Getting space is really hard when we're together all the time. But everyone needs it." Rowers therefore like to confide in people who understand the situation but are distanced from it. If for no other reason, this is where men friends on the team, or on other teams, are especially appreciated. As confidants, they can help release the tensions without touching the crew solidarity. Virtually all the women on the team have a male confidant on another English-speaking country's team — American, Australian, British, New Zealand. But athletes have to take care not to support others so much that it hurts their own concentration.

"At the Olympics and the Worlds, it's a lot easier just to stick to yourselves," says Kevin. "It's part of focusing. If you talk to someone else, they bring you down or change your focus, and you know, it's a lot easier to go back and play euchre."

During her first summer on the team, one athlete scrawled in capital letters in her journal: "I feel like screaming because there is no one to talk to here who understands me. I don't feel secure enough with anyone here to let down my defences and make myself vulnerable. Two and a half months is a long time to keep silent." Over time, athletes build support systems. They learn when to confide in their teammates and when not to. They cannot afford to share all their vulnerabilities with their crewmates. At the same time, however, nurturing each other in hard times contributes to crew solidarity.

In 1987, just before racing in Lucerne, Jenny Walinga, a member of the coxed four, hurt her back. Back injuries are very serious. An injured back can destroy a summer season for a rower and her crew, to say nothing of a possibly ruined career. With backs, it's hard to tell whether to wait for recovery, row through it or put the team spare in the crew. Everyone feels insecure. Jenny was given daily physio treatment — ice packs, heat pads, ultrasound, massage, mobilizations, manipulations, anti-inflammatories, painkillers and a couple of days' rest. When she returned to rowing with the crew, she was very careful. But still, halfway through practice her back would go into acute spasm.

"I was sitting in bow behind Jenny in two seat," remembers Heather. "After ten days, Jenny was tired of feeling like an invalid. She wasn't admitting how hurt she still was, because she wanted to be a trooper. She didn't want to let the crew down by getting behind. But I could tell things were bad by the way she was rowing. Kathryn Barr, in three seat, heard Jenny gasping in pain during our warm-up. Kathryn was so worried about Jenny that she had tears in her eyes when she turned around. 'Are you okay?' she asked. Jenny said tersely, 'I'm fine.'

"I called Drew over. 'Drew, you should take Jenny out of the boat for this practice. Don't you remember what happened to the quad last year with Silken?' Silken's back injury caused her crew to miss their final at the 1986 Worlds, and it took Silken a year to shake the injury. 'Be quiet, Heather,' Drew said. I was really angry at him for that. Didn't he remember a few days earlier, when Jenny had crumpled on the dock with her back in spasm? She had had to be helped just to walk. I was ready to jump out of the boat and swim for shore, just to make sure we didn't try to do racing pieces.

"Then Lesley, our coxswain, spoke up. Her voice shook, but she convinced Jenny that we'd all be happier if we could just row to the dock. After we got in, I went to the bathroom. While I was in there, I thought, 'Oh no. I'm going to cry.' I stayed there for so long that Lisa and Andrea found me, and then they went to get Tina. Meanwhile my crew was waiting outside to start a meeting. Tina and Lisa assured me that Drew was really good about taking people out of the boat when they said they were injured. That made me feel a lot better. Meanwhile poor Jenny thought I was mad at her because she was injured. I wasn't — I was just really worried that she was risking permanent injury.

"At our meeting, Drew decided that we should take the afternoon off. We needed a break. But the day's sorrows hadn't ended. After that practice Jane phoned home to St. Catharines for some comfort from her mother. Mrs. Tregunno reluctantly told her that Winston, the family dog, was sick. She couldn't tell her the truth — that he had already been put to sleep. Jane was devastated. More weeping.

"We all needed to take care of each other. Away from our families and other friends, we were all the support each other had. Lesley and I decided to cheer everyone up. First we arranged professional massages for all of us. Then we picked the restaurant where we would eat dinner. Then we bought material to make matching racing suits for our crew. That afternoon during the massages, we took everyone's measurements and designed our suits. The black lycra was patterned with a large white polar bear. We sewed the suits so the bear was strategically placed on our backs, for people to see when we rowed. We were coming from the Great White North to race in Europe. The joke lasted all summer." The bonding worked. Jenny's back mended. The coxed four raced very well in Lucerne, winning a silver medal.

There is always one best joke each summer. In 1986 the joke also revolved around symbols on training clothes. One day in 1986, when Heather and Lisa were very frustrated in the double and didn't have anything to laugh about, something happened. Heather was staying at the home of a history professor who was writing a book about the Far East.

"We went to Heather's for our morning feed," remembers Lisa. "I was wearing my new T-shirt. Ted, my boyfriend, had just brought it back for me from Japan. It had three oars, with flags of Canada, China and Hong Kong on them. On seeing these flags, the professor bent forward and peered more closely, raising his hands to my chest. 'It's fascinating to think what lies behind these flags!' he said. Now, I was quite self-conscious about what lay beneath those particular flags. All I could say was a weak, 'Oh..., I see.' Heather whispered, 'Historically speaking, Lisa.' I didn't get it for a minute. Then Heather and I broke out laughing. But he still looked puzzled. He followed us to the car. We were laughing so hard we couldn't drive away. Suddenly the professor saw the joke and threw his head back in laughter. For the rest of the summer, we were reduced to helpless giggles whenever we thought of it. It was the comic relief we needed."

Bonds in a crew are pragmatic. The bottom line is speed. The athletes have to be selfish in that regard. "You have to be out there for yourself to make yourself as strong as you can be," says Silken, who practises what she preaches. "But having all the women pushing to get better improves the whole team. In that way you make a contribution to the team, by working together — let's make this a good training environment." The way athletes show they care about their teammates is by trying their best to beat them. They develop mutual respect. When they feel like slacking off in a tough practice or three-quarters of the way through the race, they don't. They don't because they have too much respect for their teammates to let them down that way. Their dreams are in each other's hands. Soul as a crew.

"If you started out being competitive at an early date," says Cathy Lund, "and then formed a crew out of the people you competed against, you were almost closer. Competing with and against the other person — having this continual change in relationship — makes you wonder what these people are really like. And then it was so much fun, because there was liking and respect there." For Cathy that kind of friendship was the best part: "Without the fun of the crew, I would never have kept on rowing."

Rowing is so demanding that people cannot do it and not bond with their crewmates, to some degree. They have to get up every morning regardless of the weather or how tired they are, and go out there and perform, and hurt. They can't just go through the motions. They experience together the highs of the great pieces that punctuate practices like exclamation marks. As soon as they make sacrifices like that for the crew, or have those wonderful shared moments, they bond, no matter how different they are. The bonding is for survival and for identity, folk memory. Crews bond in and through the ups and downs of daily practice. It takes all eight to make an eight go fast. The common

framework of suffering, triumph and experience causes its sur-
vivors to say to one another, "Yeah, I know you. I know what
you're like when you're down, as well as what you're like when
you feel pretty good about yourself." Team members in any walk
of life need to know one another like that so that when the going
gets tough, they will know, trust, that the others will be there.

7

THE LEGACY

Carla Pace tightened the four screws holding her rigger to the boat. Her crew had already unloaded their boat from the trailor, put the seats back in the slides and unpacked the blades. Carla was looking forward to that afternoon's race. The Vancouver Rowing Club eight she was stroking was a strong crew, comprised entirely of former and current national team oarswomen. They were racing at the second Royal Victoria Boat Race in June 1987. Spectators and tourists milled around the inner harbour in downtown Victoria, in front of the Empress Hotel, inspecting the athletes and their equipment.

"Oh, you're fixing the boat. Isn't it nice that the ladies are involved!" said a voice above Carla's head as she bent over her rigger. Carla looked up and saw a middle-aged couple beaming at her. She pushed back a strand of her strawberry-blonde hair and smiled. "Oh, thanks."

"I'm sure the men will be pleased you're fixing the boat for them," said the woman approvingly.

"No," replied Carla, in a very polite voice, "we're racing too." When the couple left, she momentarily stared dumbfoundedly after them. Then she started to laugh, and shrieked to her crew, "Did you hear that?!" Except that they held wrenches, the women in the crew did not resemble mechanics. They all wore the sleek tights and racing jerseys of athletes.

In 1987 the women were included in the racing and the festivities at the Victoria Boat Race for the first time. All the athletes were treated royally, until it came time to go home. Then the Vancouver women discovered that they did not rate first-class treatment on their own. They went home earlier than the Vancouver men, who were staying in Victoria for a few days to train. The men's coach refused to give the women a share of the ferry money to travel from Victoria to Vancouver. That may just have been him, but when they approached the regatta organizer, she couldn't find any money for them either. Meanwhile, Cambridge and Oxford had received full funding to fly from Britain, and Harvard from Boston.

In Canada, rowing is less exclusively an elite sport than it is in the United States or, particularly, in Britain. The backbone of Canadian rowing is the community-based St. Catharines Rowing Club. St. Catharines has set the standard for equality for women and for participants from all social levels, which other city clubs in the country imitate. Young people from city high schools, as well as from private schools, compete. St. Catharines hosts the Canadian Henley Regatta, the biggest regatta in the world and a true rowers' regatta. Yet despite its relative equality, women's rowing in Canada has a different status than the men's.

Say the word "rowing" and it conjures up a clear image. Bronzed young men. Hard work and discipline. But also, sunrises over beautiful lakes where eights silently skim the water, where the only noise is the coxswain's voice, calling like a gull. For the 150 years of its existence as a college sport, rowing has meant becoming a man and entering the elite — Cambridge, Harvard and Yale — with the ensuing responsibilities and privileges. Even in the 1980s, when the sport of rowing is much more widespread than ever before, it still retains that elite image. A cohesive model is still presented to men who row. Excelling in the sport sets them up to succeed in life. Why? Because it teaches them to compete, fitting them for corporate life after they retire from rowing. Competitiveness is a male virtue.

There is a slight intimation that women disrupt the image of crew. "On the one hand," observed Tina, "rowing is a gentleman's pastime, taking place in a pastoral setting among the elite. On the other, the women who participate are assumed to be amazons of grotesque proportions who live only for their sport. Women athletes are becoming less of an anomaly in what has been a male arena of sport, but crew is not a sport where women have been easily accepted."

In 1970 the World Championships were held in St. Catharines. As part of the festivities, Jane Tregunno's parents held a reception for the FISA (Fédération Internationale de la Société d'Aviron) officials. A Dutch official named Nellie Gamble remarked that in Russia women were rowing. Eight-year-old Jane thought, "Yecch! Women rowing!" Rowing was not a sport for women, it was a sport for men. However, women started rowing internationally in 1973.

The last fifteen years have spawned a rowing experience for women that has certainly known as much joy, sorrow, bad and good luck as the men have known in the same time. But a difference exists between men's and women's rowing. Women's rowing does not have the tradition, the history of participation and therefore the clout that men's does. Thus, it is handicapped by its lack of status. Although women's rowing is growing in Canada, and thousands of women participate, fewer women than men try rowing for fun. A few women start rowing because their fathers did it. Scores of men row because their fathers did. Fewer women take rowing up seriously at the club, varsity or international level. While rowing is currently a preppy thing for co-ed undergraduates to do, they are often reluctant to commit themselves totally to it. The University of Victoria's rowing program is a happy exception. There, the women's program is very large and competitive. Al Morrow, the head coach at UVic and in 1988 a women's national team coach, is scrupulously fair in ensuring that all the athletes get good coverage. But elsewhere, most women are content to row novice or junior varsity so that they can get a crew jacket and enjoy the parties.

"For the 1988 Olympic team we are fortunate to have a small group of truly high-performance oarswomen," says Drew Harrison. "But it's a weakness that we don't have a big group. If we had twenty top people, coaches could make all kinds of mistakes and we'd still go fast. You know — kick them out because they don't smile right; then because you've still got so many people you can stick in, the boat still goes fast. But we don't have that luxury."

Why? Because fewer women take up rowing seriously and stick to it over the long term. The ratio of men to women is about 60:40 at the club level and 50:50 in high school competition, but it drops off badly after the initial stages. The lower rate of women's participation is reflected at the top. At the Olympics, the women have six races, which is only two fewer events than the men, and those events are for small boats. But at the Pan American Games and for World Lightweight Rowing, the men have an eight race while the women do not. With less opportunity for women to compete at all levels, less effort goes into the development of oarswomen at the club, varsity or international level. The lesser interest of women in rowing is a self-perpetuating problem. Solving it is as difficult as solving similar inequalities that women meet in the work force. Opening up special opportunities for women to compete — taking affirmative action — can seem like overcompensation. If the talent is not there, goes the counter-argument, why should money be wasted trying to push people up to a standard they cannot meet? But how will women, who everyone agrees are starting behind, gain equal place if they do not receive encouragement?

Not all of the women are politically aware. Several national team members had dinner together in London, Ontario, on the night of the first Royal Victoria Boat Race, in 1986. They had been feeling tired and depressed that day from a long run of training, and decided to baby themselves. They barbequed steak and mushrooms and finished off the meal with whipped cream and ice cream on top of strawberry shortcake. Over dessert the conversation turned to the boat race. The women exclaimed at the exclusion of women from the racing. Cambridge, Oxford and Harvard men were all there, along with Vancouver and Victoria contingents. Why were the women not there? They were national team members after all. One would *assume* that they were as capable of good racing as varsity men! In the middle of the discussion Marilyn Campbell said earnestly, "Can you believe it? They forgot to invite Yale!"

The other women looked at her in disbelief. "They what?"

"They forgot Yale. Harvard, Cambridge and Oxford were all invited, and not Yale." The women groaned.

"That's not the point," said Heather. "They forgot all the women."

Marilyn was coming to the matter from a different perspective than Heather. Marilyn had done a lot of fund-raising to get the Victoria Rowing Club off the ground. She knew the difficulties of marketing and looked at the situation pragmatically. The argument for not including a race for women's eights in 1986 was that the women did not have a marketable image in the view of Victoria's businesses. It was a great triumph for the Victoria Rowing Club that it had persuaded the city to participate in mounting the regatta and that it entertained the British and American crews so well. But it is a sad comment on Canadian attitudes that other countries' elite universities are more marketable than Canada's own national women's team.

The women's exclusion on the basis of marketability points up the handicap that women's rowing suffers under. Oarsmen have a glamorous image. Oarswomen do not. Although image is the last thing rowers think about once they are committed to the sport, it is a consideration for people going out to try it. The somewhat glamorous and therefore marketable sports for women are gymnastics, tennis, swimming, skiing, figure skating, track. The women who do those are seen as graceful, slender, beautiful. They sell perfume, feminine hygiene, shampoo, milk. What do women rowers sell? Nothing.

At Cambridge University in England, the women's rowing team can't get enough money to cover expenses even during the school year, let alone travel to Victoria. Meanwhile, they watch the men's team enjoy team dinners mounted by private sponsors three times every week during term. A major sponsor of the team is the food company, Danepak. Danepak did an advertisement with the Cambridge men, sporting Danepak T-shirts, grouped around a plate of ham, holding forks and looking hungry. The question is — who wants to see big healthy women tucking into ham?

Meanwhile, the publicity following the Oxford and Cambridge races more than repays the sponsors for their trouble. Thus, sponsors have been known to reward the Cambridge oarsmen for the mere fact of coming to the regattas. In September of 1987, shortly before sponsored trips to Belgium and Hungary, a Cambridge University men's eight went to Tokyo. They got happi coats, calculators, ties, tie clips and track suits for failing to make the finals of the Japanese National Championships. "It's not fair," admits one Cambridge oarsman, "but I think rowing is helped by having these trips. We are the ambassadors of the sport, not just the university. And it's fun."

Heather and Jane were ambassadors of women's rowing in 1981. Heather was not sure that she liked it. The coxed four was one of eight women's crews in two events (the double and the coxed four) invited to participate the first year women raced in the Royal Henley Regatta in Britain. They were guests, and therefore outsiders. They were invited to race in an exhibition race. They saw the men in their boaters and club-crested blazers, the women in their long dresses and full-brimmed hats. The gentlemen and ladies set up picnic tables against their Rolls Royces, and spread out their china on their linen tablecloths. In the steward's enclosure the athletes heard the gentlemen explaining the basics of rowing, as they understood them, to their ladies. The spectators clapped their hands together as the crews went by, exclaiming, "Well rowed, chaps! Well rowed." All so dignified. These same old chivalrous gentlemen could not allow Heather's crew to pass by carrying their boat without volunteering to do it for them. The offers sounded absurd.

"It was very exciting to be there," explains Heather, "but I resented the implication that it was a special privilege for us. I felt we deserved it. It also irked me that they were making such a big to-do about something that we had done every day, for years — that is, getting in a boat and rowing. It was as if by recognizing women in rowing we suddenly existed. Had they not noticed that women had already rowed in two Olympics?"

"What's it like to be a woman?" asked a British journalist at the Royal Henley Regatta. Heather didn't know how she should answer. "What a stupid question," she thought, but responded, "I beg your pardon?" She supposed he was referring to what it was like being a woman at an event previously reserved for men. "We felt like we were on exhibit. They were so curious about us. We were always the centre of attention and couldn't stretch out without people snapping pictures and wanting to feel our muscles."

The women's events at the Royal Henley were discontinued after 1982. "At the Henley," says Rudy, "I think the reasons for including the women were wrong, and I was glad when they stopped. I think the English are among the world's biggest poppycocks when it comes to male chauvinism. The English Henley is one of the most out-of-date regattas."

Some fifty years ago, Jack Kelly, the father of Princess Grace of Monaco, was not awarded the trophy he deserved for winning the double sculls at the Royal Henley. He was only a bricklayer from Philadelphia, not a gentleman. However, it seems that amends were made the year Heather and Jane competed at the Royal Henley Regatta; Princess Grace awarded the medals to winners of the women's double — Canadians Lisa Wright (Roy) and Janice Mason.

The assumption that rowing means male and elite, although less prevalent in Canada, is still strong. In 1982 Canada did not have a national men's sweep team. However, some of the men's Olympic hopefuls trained together at the Hanlan Boat Club in Toronto. They were written up in Toronto papers as an elite group and, in truth, there *was* only one man not from private school in the eight. But that one, Stephen Beatty, who came from Woodstock, Ontario, resented an article about the unfairness of this crew winning the Canadian Henley Regatta. The article implied that the reason they won was that they were all privileged and didn't have to work. This was not true in Stephen's case and he wanted credit for that. He was given credit among the men — half in earnest they called him "The Champion." However, he liked the status of rowing with a very powerful group of people. Stephen profited from that image.

Most likely the other members of the crew were offended too by the implication that they didn't have to work. They worked damn hard pulling on that oar. Rowers idealize hard work, and indeed that's the way to win. In that sense rowing is a meritocracy. The cream rises to the top. But there's more to it than that. For those men, that elite mentality — believing that they really were the best — would carry over into the rest of their lives. According to Stephen, "The men from the 1982-88 period are the perfect old boys' network. In thirty years they will all surface at the top, for they come from the same background. Even if they don't, they still have access by telephone to the power, because they proved they could pull on an oar and be the best." Many men who row do not come from an elite background, but they all can profit from the image if they want to.

Women can use rowing as a vehicle for upward mobility the same way men can. One oarswoman said about her teammates, "They're not from privileged backgrounds. They see privilege in rowing, and they want it." The women on the 1988 national team do just fine — they tend to come from middle-class backgrounds and almost all have university degrees. But the difference has been there. And on the whole, women's rowing has only the image that derives from the facts — that the women have to be big and strong and committed. These qualities are more often than not caricatured, as Tina pointed out when she said that oarswomen have an image as grotesque, driven amazons. The women are caricatured because people are still uneasy about women who display the "manly virtues."

While they are respected, oarswomen are considered unusual women, rather than ideal women. They do not receive the unqualified approval for being competitive and strong that men do. While men who row move on to become power-brokers, according to the image, no one knows yet what women rowers are likely to do when they stop rowing. For example, Tricia Smith competed in the first Olympics for women in rowing and still rows on the national team. She has just started her career as a lawyer. Though she is pursuing a route followed by generations of oarsmen, she has few female models for it. Whatever she does, she will be forging new ground as a woman.

Many of the oarsmen think that one reason the women don't get the same approval as men is because they are not accomplishing as much as the men are. They argue that since fewer women row, there is less competition and therefore a victory is less significant. This attitude nips at the women's heels, all the way up the rowing pyramid. It is true that on every level — club, varsity and international — there are usually fewer crews in women's races than there are in men's. Consequently, at every level there is less depth. But the individual top oarswomen at each level work as hard as their male counterparts. These women are respected as individuals for what they do. Nonetheless, they are seen as exceptions. At the University of Western Ontario the oarsmen nicknamed the women "The Bettys," using old Second World War slang for women. They liked having pretty girls around because they were fun to party with, but they didn't take them seriously as athletes. Although the Western women won consistently, and more often than the men, the men asserted that women's racing was less competitive.

In the late 1980s, though, the Canadian women have reason to be proud of their tradition at the domestic and international level. Since 1975, when women started to compete internationally in rowing, the Canadian women's senior team has won thirteen World Championship and Olympic medals. In the same time period, the Canadian men's senior team has won only six World Championship and Olympic medals. The women won bronze medals in the eight in 1977 and 1978, and also bronze and silver in the pair, while the men's program languished medalless at the side of the picture. The reason the men have improved so much more recently is because their program was rigorously developed over the 1980s. Like many people, Doug Hamilton opines that since the late '70s was the initial stage of women's rowing, it was easier to win medals then. In the 1980s "the standard of world women's rowing has risen — cutting off three to four seconds per year. No individual athlete can make that improvement at the top level, year after year. The Canadian women have basically held their own, but their relative position has declined." Tricia, who was on the women's team in the 1970s and has continued to win medals in the 1980s, feels there's more to it than relative performance.

"We learned so much in the Seventies," she says. "We had some excellent coaches. It is all relative, and maybe they didn't know as much as the coaches do now. But I think I had a lot of advantages. There was a really good group of people that trained together in Vancouver, under a really good technical taskmaster. We worked and progressed together. We didn't have to be there, we just wanted to. We had a lot of fun. Some of the women who started after me didn't have the coaches and opportunities I had, since some key coaches left the country, so women's rowing was not progressing as quickly as it could have. Because the women trained together less, too, I felt there was a lull for a while."

Part of the success of the Canadian women in the initial years was a result of particularly good coaching. Among others, Kris Korzeniowski coached the Canadian women's team in 1976 and 1977. One of team members, Joy Fera, recalls Kris saying to them, "You'll never be as big as the Russians. So you just have to row better." He capitalized on their strong points as technicians and assessed their weak points honestly. Tricia says that "Kris was an incredible coach. We'd do exercises to improve our rowing technique for kilometre after kilometre. It really developed our confidence in each other in terms of our skill. We could put a boat together in any combination with the people that learned then." Tina had Kris as coach at Princeton. She agrees with Tricia. "He has such a record of coaching success in so many different countries and different levels. As an athlete for Poland, too, he was phenomenal. I really respect his ability to convey his perfectionism in style, in performance. He never gives you a moment's rest until you perfect your stroke." Kris left Canada to take the Princeton coaching job in 1977 because no full-time position existed in Canada. After several years there he went to coach in Italy. Shortly thereafter he was appointed the U.S. coach. His men's eight won the World Championship gold in 1987. Although the Canadian women have had good coaches since Kris left, they still remember those days.

Adding insult to the view that the women's medals of the Seventies were more easily won, is the injury that the men's success is more recent. The women have won only five medals since 1984, while the men have won six. On top of that, two of the men's medals are gold, one an Olympic gold, while the women's are silver and bronze. As Drew Harrison, the current women's coach, noted, "If a few of our individuals win gold medals at the Olympics, a lot of people are going to feel the sense of having it all."

Canadian men's rowing has certainly performed a dazzling about-face in the 1980s. The Seventies, when the women were doing so well, were "the dark ages of men's rowing in Canada," according to Mel LaForme.

Mel paid his dues on the men's team through the 1970s. He was a member of the men's eight in 1980 — a crew that protested their dismal situation graphically. First they tried to dump their coach and held so many meetings to discuss solutions that the women called them the Olympic Meeting Team. Next, after disappointing performances in Europe, they were not allowed to race at the English Henley. In protest they removed the Canadian flags from their oars at the Amsterdam regatta in June 1980. All the athletes retired from the sweep program. One, Peter Mac-Gowan, who had switched to sculling to avoid the ill-fated sweep team, made a presentation to the Board of Directors in 1982. He demanded that the athletes' needs be given more consideration. His activism coincided with efforts by the administration to address the problem by promoting development. By 1984, the men's program had turned around. One astonished oarswoman says, "All of a sudden you had all of these guys crawling out of the woodwork that I'd never heard of, and two years later they were winning a gold medal." In 1985 Mel LaForme won his first World Championship medal, a gold in the men's quad, then followed it with bronzes in 1986 and 1987.

Since the men have had this success in the 1980s — and from a superficial perspective had more distance to come than the women's program did in the decade — the women find it hard to avoid a superficial comparison and feel that something is wrong. As Tina says, " I think people nowadays see the women's program as being discontented, always complaining. What they don't see is that maybe we had some ground to break, which was why we've had to challenge so much. Maybe we're making the paths of the new people easier." And in actual fact, the men as well as the women have been active to secure athletes' rights as the new Canadian sport system has been set in place during the 1980s. Together the men and women have worked to clarify selection and appeal procedures.

But the women have had more work to do on their own than the men. With the initial flush of excitement about the beginning of women's rowing over, the women have tried to institutionalize their place in the sport, encountering problems like uneven coaching and allocation of facilities. Although it is changing, generally more and better coaches prefer to coach men's than women's crews. The good women's programs that have existed at the club and national level have been the work of keen individuals and have usually dropped off when those individuals left. Men's programs, meanwhile, exist at clubs as a given. "The difference shows in equipment use," observes Kay. "Who gets what boats. Something's not valid unless a man corroborates it. Also, it seems like men's heavyweight rowing is *the* answer.

More men do row, but it seems like women's rowing is *only* women's rowing."

As far as national team rowing goes, Sport Canada follows a policy of equitability. That means that where opportunites exist for women to compete, they will get the same amount of money. In 1988 the high-performance budget for Lucerne and the Olympics is about a million dollars. There are two-thirds as many women as men on the team, depending on which crews qualify, so the women will receive about 40 per cent of the funding.

The problem in women's national team rowing is the development of athletes. Most of the emphasis in development in the 1980s has been on the men, simply because in 1980 the women's team was riding high internationally and the men's was in a slump. But in the effort to bring the men up to the women's level and the excitement over their success, further women's development was overlooked. Jim Joy, speaking for Rowing Canada, admits that "the coverage in the development area for men may have been stronger, with the work of Boris Klavora and Al Morrow in Vancouver and Victoria in those years. I think that's a hard fact. A number of innovations in the national team rowing program since 1981, beginning with the Senior B, were initially only done with the men. In the period between 1983 and 1986 there has not been a good record of development for the women." New women are being encouraged in 1988, and they will go to the Olympics if they do well enough in Lucerne. But some oarswomen feel that such an effort would have been better made two years ago.

The lull in women's development in the early 1980s is coming home to roost in the late 1980s. There are too few women near top calibre behind the present national team members. In the early 1980s, a gap opened in women's development when Rudy went to the national team, when Doug Clark went to Boston and when Ted Daigneault left UVic. Some other coaches have since been bringing women along, but as Rudy says, "there hasn't been that influx of new talent. Maybe the interest isn't there. People can chastise me because I had the high school approach, but part of that was developing people. And the high school approach isn't there now, and where's the development? Where's the beef?"

There is some beef, but not much. One former national team oarswoman, Kathy Lichty, who rowed on the team from 1977 to 1985, is now coaching in St. Catharines. "I've got someone training for me who's pulling a high erg and is rowing pretty well. She'll do anything. But how is she ever going to break into the international level? There's no intermediate level. Unfortunately, she's the beginning of the new. How do I break her in? They're keeping the team so small these days. Which is a good thing because you don't want to send people over to the Worlds if there's not the depth. But what do you do? Most of the girls aren't inspired."

As a top athlete in 1985, Tina was sensitive to the discrepancy between her experience in 1981-82, when she fought to make the team, and that of the new candidates. "In 1985-86 so many people just walked on to the team who didn't experience trying and trying and trying to make it when the competition was really fierce, having to put everything on the line just to make the team and then having to focus on going to the Worlds. I'm not advocating that, but the real sense of pride — in making the team, in your performance, in the women who have come before you — it's something we have that the younger women don't. But it's impossible to pass that on to people."

Pride in oneself and one's team may take time to develop. Unlike Tina, Kay made the national team eight in 1981 on her first attempt. Kay had not proved to herself that she was really good. Could the team be that good if she were on it? In 1988, after trying to break into the medals for seven years, Kay has a healthy respect for the challenge. Nevertheless, the lack of depth reinforces the disdain felt by any oarsmen or established oarswomen who have forgotten that they may have "walked on." Those old soldiers remember the jostle and fight on the way up. The maturing oarswomen might shy away from competition that is surprisingly stiff at the top of the Canadian ladder, not being used to the fight, since they do not have much competition after they reach the top of the club and varsity level. When Heather returned to competition in 1986 after a year of retirement, one national team hopeful asked her, "Why are all the old girls coming back?" "She didn't think it was fair," recalls Heather, "and said that she thought it was time that we moved over for the younger people. I told her that she could have my seat anytime she beat me. But it made me think she wasn't competitive. When I started going for the national team, I was inspired by the very fact of competing against silver and bronze medallists."

The success of the women's team in the late 1970s gave them a strong sense of pride, and generated interest. Kathy Lichty remembers that, on making the team for the first time in 1977, "the boat was all veterans and I was just shaking in my boots. I just followed. I pulled. I had great respect. In 1979 I couldn't believe I made the top boat — I made it and thought, 'These guys are good.'" Jim Joy concurs that "once you have a lot of success it would accelerate the development process for the next quadrennial." He feels that "with the right placement of these athletes now, the women's team will shock the world at Seoul. I see the development thing as turning around, say before 1992."

Jim sees beyond the assumption that success will breed success: "It's really a priority in my mind to improve the women's program." Which is a good thing, because the women still fight an uphill battle. Their lack of tradition hurts them. Since rowing for them is relatively recent, they still need to stake out ground for themselves. They don't have generations preceding them to legitimize their rowing the way the men do. Fortunately, though, the first generation of national team women from the 1970s are now carrying the torch out to more people. Susan Antoft, who won two World medals in the pair, is putting together a presentation to publicize women's rowing, and she plans to take it to high schools across the country. There is a new newsletter called *Women Pulling Together.* But still, as Doug Clark says, "There's not much structure or recruiting. Women's rowing is certainly not a high priority, in the development end of it, in Canada. There are a limited number of good coaches in Canada and the majority of them still gravitate towards the men." Many ex-oarswomen, like Carol Love in Peterborough and Kathy Lichty in St. Catharines, are now becoming coaches, which is a strong step forward in the development of women's rowing. Doug is eager to help, too. "I want to be part of it. I see far more challenge in the women's program because it hasn't been done yet."

Despite these improvements, however, women don't get the encouragement men do to row or take up any physically demanding activity — inside or outside of the sport world. This lack of positive reinforcement holds them back, conditioned as they are to look for approval. Carla Pace retired after stroking the Vancouver eight in the 1987 Royal Victoria Boat Race. She had been on and off both sculling and sweep national teams since 1981. She comments: "In this quadrennial no one ever told us that we were any good, never gave us any encouragement. And then they wonder why the women on the team have a problem with succeeding and why they are afraid of sacrificing everything for rowing. When I was coaching at the Florida Rowing School in 1986, I was in a totally different atmosphere. The Americans idolize their athletes, and I was told how neat my rowing was, all the time. As a result of that support, that feedback, I performed better."

At present, in Canada, the women rely almost exclusively on each other for support and feedback. Yet there is infinitely more at issue in this situation than an American/Canadian difference in treatment of celebrities. Women in Western society are not encouraged to do sports that emphasize strength or size. Women who do those sports are respected, but they are seen as different from the norm. Whether or not they care to be considered normal, they set themselves apart from the mainstream, especially if they pursue their sport seriously. The only people they will receive unqualified support from are their peers in the sport. Men who pursue sport seriously are of course apart from the mainstream as well, but they are heroes, the epitome of their society's ideals; the women, though lauded, may be viewed almost suspiciously as freaks of nature. The difference is crucial.

"Oarswomen got almost no positive feedback outside the rowing community, and probably got lots of implied negative feedback," says Gordon Gwynne-Timothy, a Canadian oarsman who rowed at both Harvard and Cambridge universities. "They hung around with each other all the time, a very close group. We oarsmen hung around with each other a lot too, but as a group we more often had other social milieux. That applied to dating, too. Oarswomen mostly only went out with male rowers. Male rowers went out with everyone. Maybe women are more into the rowing 'culture' than men are because it put them into — I guess you could call it a 'subculture,' or at least a more ambiguous position — while it put us at the top of the mainstream of Harvard culture. If anything, rowing was the 'superculture.'"

As teenagers and young adults, oarsmen can play at life-and-death competition and develop the appropriate male attributes of intense focus, self-discipline and ruthlessness. They form bonds with their teammates, learning to trust one another in the shared moments of pressure and fun that are a rehearsal for life in the world of career competition. As members of the "superculture" of sport, they are seen as "supermen." Although Canadian men's rowing is by no means the same as rowing at Harvard, any good men's crew can relate to the following sentiment. "When I was in the first freshman eight," recalls Gordon, "any theme our coach had as we approached our final race, if there was a theme, was that we were the best. We had complete certainty that we were better than anyone else — better coach, we tried harder, trained longer. Simply, we were the balls."

By contrast, if oarswomen truly excel in competition, in ruthlessness and in strength, they are being something the traditional female is not. In the late twentieth century, the traditional sex archetypes are being rethought, and that includes widening the scope of "femininity" to include the active qualities, as well as not limiting men to being macho. But traditional knee-jerk reactions are strong. Rowing, like all sports, is "part of becoming a man." Hence a fundamental ambivalence about what the ramifications of rowing are for women. When asked her opinion on the topic, Tricia said, "I haven't really thought about it in those terms. You certainly get the sense of an old boy network in work as well as in sport. I can see how that flows over. Certainly it's something that men really identify with, it's a topic of conversation like any other thing that's unusual about you. In that respect, I can see that women don't really have the same thing. Rowing doesn't make us 'women.'"

8

PINK SHIRTS AND POWER

At 7 a.m. on a dark grey morning in late August 1983, the Canadian women's team were at the course in Duisburg, West Germany. They had had the racecourse to themselves for a few days, being the first country to arrive at the site of the World Championships. The women's eight took their boat and blades down to the dock and prepared to go out on the water. Once in the boat, they paused briefly to tie their feet into their footstops and remove their jackets. Then they called out their seat numbers from bow to stroke to let the coxswain know they were ready to shove off. "All eight, ready, push!" called the cox. As the eight left the dock, they heard whistles and exclamations from the American men's team, who were rounding the corner of the boathouse. The Americans were always so extroverted — hard to miss.

"Get a load of those pink shirts! Hoo-wee! You girls trying to make a political statement or something?" The calm of the early morning was broken.

Getting a reaction was fun, but the Canadian women had not expected this one. The pink shirts had seemed innocuous enough in the Cotton Ginny store where they bought them. A coxswain on the team worked at Cotton Ginny's and could get them a deal. Eight extra-large and one extra-small shirt, all identical, proved hard to find. Tina and Sarah Ogilvie, the two crew appointees for getting training gear, had sleuthed about for a while. In the end, they'd had to get two slightly different styles. The eight women jostled for the roomier ones.

"It was by chance that we got pink shirts in 1983," recalls Angie, "because it was the only colour they had nine in. But the pink did make a striking combination. We rowed a black and white zebra-striped boat and wore black tights. We got a great deal of attention, which we didn't mind." However, reactions were mixed. Angie recounts, "One of the American women came up to me and said, 'What's the pink for? Is that in case someone doubts?' I knew she meant my sexuality. And I said, 'No, it's to distract you at the starting gates.' Throwing it back at her. But it was a serious thing."

In 1985 the American women's quad had T-shirts printed up with "Women's Straight Quad" in big letters on the back. The year 1985 was the first time women did not have a coxswain in the quad. A boat without a coxswain is called a "straight" boat, that is, straight four as opposed to coxed four. The men race both the straight and the coxed four, while traditionally the women have raced only the coxed four, the theory being that women can't steer and row at the same time. In fact, the women were happy to be rid of the coxswain's weight. A straight quad is much faster. An eight needs a coxswain — it goes so fast, it needs someone facing forward to steer. And with eight people there has to be a leader. More significant for the women in the American quad in 1985, though, was the *double-entendre* of the designation on their shirts. Those women were straight — that is, they were heterosexual.

Many men were giving the American women a wide berth because a few in fact were lesbian. Most were not. But in any case, it was offensive that sexual orientation should be an issue at all. Rowers come to regattas to race. That oarswomen are measured by any standard other than their expertise as rowers, is inexcusable. But they are measured by irrelevant standards — by society, by male rowers and sometimes by each other.

"The way many of the U.S. women decided to be taken seriously was to act like men," observed Angie in the aftermath of the pink shirt conversation in 1983. "They deserve a lot of respect as athletes. But they didn't need to give up being women. Giving up being women defeats the purpose of gaining respect as a woman. I think the point is to be a woman and to be taken seriously." But have the Canadian women been taken seriously? The American response to Angie's comment has been, "If the Canadian women would stop worrying about being women, they would be faster."

When the Canadian women wore pink shirts in Duisburg, they sent a message to the Americans saying that they were feminine. That message, although unintended, was significant. It created confusion. What did femininity matter in the rowing context? Was it even appropriate, given that femininity traditionally means passive, dependent, submissive? To succeed in rowing, athletes must be aggressive, competitive and physically strong. These are traditionally male — not female — attributes. When the Canadian women realized that wearing pink was political, they started thinking about what the pink shirts meant. When they got inappropriate responses from people and were judged as pretty rather than powerful rowers, they discovered that the two — attractiveness and strength — did not necessarily mesh.

Women are forging new identities as serious athletes. Over the last fifteen years, with strong women both inside and outside sport, oarswomen have been redefining "femininity" to include the attributes of competitiveness, single-mindedness and size. Because of the fitness boom, strong and fit is not unusual for women in wider society in 1988. But big and very strong still is. Thus, oarswomen, more than women in many other sports, challenge social norms.

How much the women have to challenge depends on the local standard. "Canadian men and women are historically more on par in the rowing world than the American men and women have been," observes Nancy Storrs, a former American national team member now living in Canada. Thus, for better or for worse, Canadian men's and women's rowing is more integrated. The Canadians have always had one national rowing association. Men's and women's races at the club and collegiate level are held together. In the United States, by contrast, the women have had a separate rowing association from the men's, and 1987 was the first year the men's and women's U.S. National Championships were held together. The American oarswomen have a more radical history than their Canadian counterparts, primarily because the elite male rowing tradition is much stronger in the United States than it is in Canada.

"The U.S. women had to fight to get recognition and status," says Nancy. Widespread women's rowing started at the collegiate level in the early 1970s. Princeton University became a co-ed university in 1970, and the women started rowing in 1971-72. Still, the men fought their invasion of the boathouse tooth and nail. The women got their own locker room only in 1981, although Title IX, the U.S. federal law requiring equal opportunity for women in physical and other education programs, was passed in 1972. In 1976 the Yale varsity women, who were national champions that year, stood naked on the main steps leading to the office of the president of the Yale campus. They made the point that they needed changing facilities.

"Even though Doug Clark complained about the women at the University of Western Ontario getting less funding than the men, at least the women at Western had their own toilet. At least they were allowed into the Western boathouse!" exclaims Nancy.

"Pushing hard against inequality isn't all bad, though," she continues. "The American women were really out to prove something. Every time you want to prove something, you push harder, which helps you get better." In 1984 the American women's eight won the Olympic gold medal.

Because the Canadian women have fought less overt discrimination and have also achieved good success internationally, they have not seen the need to be so radical. At the University of Western Ontario, for example, Doc Fitz-James took the personal initiative of starting the women's rowing program in the early 1970s. Doc *is* Western rowing. He has coached there for at least thirty-five years and has single-handedly kept the under-funded team afloat by buying boats himself.

However, Western oarswomen still encounter insidious discrimination. Doc, with his saturnine sense of humour, pokes fun at the lightweight men's crews all the time, although he himself rowed lightweight. Doc's disparaging comments about the women are presumably akin to the ones about lightweights. The women accept some teasing from Doc, because he is from an older generation. But they object to the oarsmen mindlessly incorporating the sexism.

"Although individually the men respected the women," says Angie, speaking of the summer of 1980, when she rowed in the Western club eight, "collectively they were like a motorcycle gang. You know, the women are only broads. When Doc felt like making us really mad one time, he called us dogs. One of the guys put a sign saying 'Doghouse' on our bathroom door. I got in a fight with Doc shortly after that. I always used to initiate the fights. I had organized the crew to take out one particular boat and he noticed and said, 'Just hold it there, you dogs,' and I said, 'Well, I'd rather be a dog than a puppy. See you later.' And all the guys were furious. They came up and said, 'How dare you insult Doc like that, in front of the guys?' They all supported him, and he called me a dog."

The attitude that women rowers are "dogs" did exist and does still surface occasionally even among the women. In 1979, Heather's first year on the national team, she was chastised by her new teammate for wearing her headband before she got into the boat. "Heather, do you want to look like a tire-biter?" Heather didn't know what her teammate meant. She had the expression explained to her. Certain oarswomen from another country wore sweatbands everywhere, and as Heather's concerned informant said, "Everyone knows they're dogs." Heather got the message. She also got the message that she should wear black tights, not (horrors) brown, and put on her Danskin under her tights. Only dancers wore the bodysuit over their tights. It was important to keep up the Canadian women's tradition of being, in their own words, fast *and* pretty.

"When I tried out for the team in 1978," says Cathy Lund, "all these humungous women were there, though it turned out they were the same size as me once I got to know them. They were all so glamorous, gorgeous and they all seemed blonde." When the Canadian rowing magazine asked in a 1978 interview, "What do you think about Canadian rowing?," the defending World champion British men's double replied, "We like the Canadian girls very much!" The Canadian women enjoyed this reputation.

"When I was training in New Zealand in 1981," says Kathy Lichty, "I met this fellow who had been a liaison for the Canadian team at the World Championships there in 1978. He said, 'Oh, the Canadians! We all voted them the best-looking team.' In the same breath he said, 'Didn't your eight win a bronze medal?' It was nice to hear that we were good-looking. Anyone likes to hear that whether they're male or female. But the Canadian girls, we danced a lot, had fun and we were nice. And we knew how to row. I don't think people ever had trouble seeing us as women and as athletes."

However, many people do have problems seeing oarswomen as both.

"My crew was insulted as athletes at the Olympics," recalls Angie. "Rudy was having his final talk with us the night before the race, and this rep from Sport Canada turned up, saying, 'Can I come in?' We were upset because Neil would never have allowed anyone in — 'Forget it, you can't talk to my boys now.' Rudy let him in. And this guy said, 'I want to let you know, girls, before you go out there, that no matter what happens we still love you.' We were furious that this man would patronize us. First 'girls' and then 'we still love you.' We were there to win. How dare this man treat us like schoolgirls! If he had ever done that to Neil's crew, they would have knocked him flat. You can't allow that way of thinking to enter in at all."

"Andrea, your haircut really suits you," the director of the selection committee had said after explaining why she had been cut from the coxed four in 1987. Jim Joy, the national team director, had piped up, "Your eye makeup looks great!" Andrea Schreiner had been furious. They'd been trying to soften the blow for her, she'd been perfectly aware of that, but she had resented their assumption that compliments on her appearance would make her feel better about her rowing performance. The committee would never have dreamed of telling a man they'd cut that he was still good looking. Yes, Andrea was a woman, but she had come to that room to be judged as an athlete. She had not been sending them a mixed message; they had given her an inappropriate response.

Until 1985 women raced 1,000 metres. Since the three-minute race required them to be very powerful, coaches put the emphasis on size. With the switch to 2,000 metres for women, cardiovascular fitness is now emphasized and thus a leaner body. But oarswomen go and always have gone far beyond the body-sculpture, twenty-minute-workout approach to fitness. In 1980, when the Olympic coach wanted the oarswomen to weigh an arbitrary 170 pounds, Kathy Lichty remembers eating a whole bowl of potatoes one night after dinner to gain weight. The oarswomen do weight programs designed to increase their maximum strength. In the weight room at Simon Fraser University in 1980, they annoyed the B.C. Lions football players, who lifted there as well. In the football players' opinion, weights weren't for women — especially these women, who on some exercises could lift almost as much as they could. One day a particularly pretty and soft-spoken member of the rowing team asked a football player if he could please give her a five-kilogram weight plate after he finished with it. He threw it at her.

Heather ate 10,000 calories a day in 1980, a few thousand calories more than her teammates ate then and much more than she eats in 1988. The team nutritionist measured everyone's caloric intake. The coach, who was concerned about Heather's size, asked her daily what her weight was. When Heather started rowing in 1976, she was a skinny 117 pounds. By the fall of 1979, she had worked up to 140 pounds of solid muscle; 170 pounds was out of reach, but she still tried. That winter she increased her strength dramatically and put on 12 more pounds in two months. Her body was responding to doing those 300-pound deadlifts. To deadlift is to squat, arms and back straight, and then lift the weight by straightening the legs. Heather's boyfriend said everyone was talking about her being on steroids. Heather's new nickname? "Staroid." That hurt Heather. Using steroids was, and still is, unacceptable to the Canadian rowers, not to mention its illegality by Olympic rules.

"The rowing environment is freer from social pressure to be skinny, but not totally," says Silken. "If you want to get strong, you have to like muscles and feel comfortable. Otherwise it can work negatively. The Canadian women's team is pretty stunning, and yet they all think they could lose ten pounds. This works against them, although it never reaches a conscious level. They don't think they are settling for second best. It is ironic."

"The problem with being fast and pretty is the weight problem," says Angie. Hers is an extreme example of the ambivalent attitude, but she speaks truly enough for other women. "There's no question that once you go under a certain weight and fat percentage you're weaker and more susceptible to being sick. In 1983 I dieted. Being pretty and knowing it can help your self-confidence unless you get distracted by wanting to lose weight. I just look at the difference in my performance from 1983 when I weighed 151 to 1984 when I was close to 170 pounds." At least in part, Angie has reservations about weight gain. In 1983, when she dieted and thought about being pretty, "I dated a lot of men, but in 1984 I left everything behind me for rowing."

All her life, Angie loved sport because that was her gift, but she consciously developed her feminine qualities. "Dad taught me how to arm-wrestle. I once arm-wrestled the boy who cleaned the stables — he was fourteen and bigger than I was, and said I was a runt. So I beat him, and my dad saw us. It was definitely technique and the fact was he was freaked out being by a woman. I used to take advantage of that a lot. Some girls on the track team and I used to go out my first year of university to bars, and scout out victims — men with big egos. We would challenge them for free drinks if I won, and I'd win. It was ball-busting at its best. I loved the power.

"My father was afraid that I would never get married because I'd never meet a man who could overpower me. I said to him, 'But Dad, you taught me how to wrestle when I was five!' There was no way I would change at sixteen from being one of the boys to ribbons and curls." She started modelling so as to assuage her father's fears. "I got the money for modelling by threatening him I would become a garage mechanic."

When Angie went to Western, she started competing in shot-put. "My father just about had tears in his eyes when on my birthday that first fall of university he found out I weighed 180 pounds and was benchpressing 175 to 180 pounds. He freaked out and said, 'I don't have a daughter anymore, I have a half-and-half.' And the lifestyle of the throwing sports is so mas-culine, it's the most masculine. But I broke the stereotype because I was a model, so I looked good even when I was heavy. It was wonderful to play off being soft and hard because you could be anything you wanted."

Oarswomen who stay in the sport over years must become comfortable with their size. Ironically, many still seem to incor-porate a belief that femininity means small into their conception of what it is to feel good about themselves as women. The 1984 Olympic champion in the single, Romanian Valeria Recila, is six feet two inches and probably 170 pounds. She is lean, graceful and darkly beautiful by any standard, and at the Olympics she received a lot of attention from the Western teams, male and female. The Canadian women admire her "because she's beauti-ful and strong and fast." She won her Olympic final by lengths and lengths.

"Yet it is a bit of a problem being in the single," says Valeria. "It was very pleasant to be Olympic champion, and like everyone else, I want to do it one more time. But when I see how big and strong the East German sculler is, I feel pessimistic because I think I might lose. Still, I wouldn't like to be bigger and stronger even if it meant being faster. It's not everything to be big and strong...and stupid!" Valeria too seems to feel that big is bad and unfeminine. She has revised the definition of "too big" enough upward so that small(er), and therefore "feminine," still includes her, big and strong though she is. The "big is bad" way of thinking is curious. Size ought not to define femininity.

"It is an interesting comment on our own socialization when, as Canadian athletes, we look at the Russian women winning the gold, and we think, negatively, 'Look at the size of them!'" says Silken, who is taking English and women's studies at the University of Western Ontario. "Instead, we should look at the power and determination that allow these athletes to be the best." The biggest women in the Russian eight, which is stacked with the top athletes, weigh over 200 pounds and are six feet three inches. They come to the World Championships to prove that they are the fastest oarswomen in the world. They compete on the water, and they should be evaluated on the water. The World Championships are not a beauty pageant.

"Those rowing models for us not only conflict with the social one," observes Silken, "but with our own rowing-community ideal. We want to be strong but we think of the disruption of our own body image." Although not all of the Canadian women have this kind of ambivalence, the feeling is there.

"I'm not saying that what the Soviets do is a bad thing," says Angie, "but many of us do not put the medal above how we feel about ourselves to the point that they do." For the Soviets, though, the equation of womanhood and sport may be different than it is for Western women. They do not have the Western media image as their standard of attractiveness. And the accomplishment of winning gold medals helps them in the other areas of their lives. It is like a kid hockey player who gets lifted into a world of untold riches when he makes the National Hockey League. Even in Communist states upward social mobility through sport exists in some measure. Former Olympic and

World champion speed skater Karen Kania negotiated in East
Germany for a larger apartment and the opportunity to take a
year off to have a child in 1985. Since the sport authorities did
not want her to retire, she got her demands.

The difference between the largest Soviets and most of the
Canadians is indeed striking.

"My first year on the team," recalls Cathy Lund, "I was creep-
ing along at 150 pounds. In 1978, at the Worlds in New Zealand,
we would sit down right next to the Russian women. My first
encounter ever was with Olga from the Russian quad, stacking
her plate with bacon. We were watching our diets because the
coaches said, 'Don't eat yourself out of a medal.' Later on, we
were in the weigh-in room, which was a separate tent. And Olga
came in and saw my pair partner on the scale. She started laughing — like, 'Look at this pipsqueak here.' When we left, we
peaked around the corner to watch as she got on the scale. And
holy smokes! Forty-three pounds difference! In your first year
you notice that more because you're so impressionable."

The Canadian women respect the Soviets a lot more than the
Canadian men do. An oarswoman on the Olympic team who is
six feet tall and 180 pounds — in the same size range as many
of the Soviets — remarks, "I was always proud of my size and
height and used it to my advantage. When I got into rowing, it
became an issue — some people were very conscious of their
size and weight. When we're in a group, people do stare at us,
and I guess it can be a little intimidating. Then you realize you
are different from the general population. But I was really
surprised when I discovered that people were so hung up about
it. I remember looking at the Russians at the Worlds and thinking, 'Boy, I'd love to be three inches taller and twenty pounds
heavier.' And yet you do go back to Canada and sometimes wish
you could be twenty pounds lighter and five inches shorter. But
it amazes me how many of the women rowers see themselves as
freaks. I've accepted my size from the beginning, although I've
gotten more conscious of it."

However, this woman harbours her own brand of ambivalence. "The introduction of lightweight women's rowing at the international level has not helped our cause at all. It makes us feel bigger. They have to starve themselves, they have very little muscle. We're the other extreme — 150 pounds and up, five feet ten inches plus. The women's rowing team was always the women's rowing team until the lightweights came along, and then we became the 'heavy' women. That's a negative word to use."

The top U.S. women's sculler, Anne Marden, is relatively small by international standards — a stocky and powerful five feet seven inches and 150 pounds. She supports lightweight women's rowing whole-heartedly, but says, half in jest, "I'm sensitive to the size issue because there's a very lean, successful lightweight rower named Anne Martin. It's just devastating, especially when people say, 'My you've put on weight!'" To add to the confusion, both Annes won bronze medals for the U.S. in the single at the 1985 Worlds.

Lightweight women's rowing began internationally in 1984. In 1985 their championships were held along with the heavyweights for the first time. The weight category for lightweight women is crew average of 125 pounds, with maximum at 130 pounds. The weight limit for lightweight men is 160 pounds, with crew average of 155 pounds. The lightweight men have had international championships for years. Because lightweight rowing is not an Olympic event, it has a different status than heavyweight rowing. In Canada, lightweights do not get carded because the funding is reserved for Olympic sports. Also, with no Olympic incentive, very few Eastern bloc countries compete in lightweight events. Thus, lightweight rowing suffers from a slight lack of prestige. But lightweight women's rowing is a particularly big deal in Canada, Britain and the United States.

Canadian Heather Hattin is the 1987 World champion in the lightweight double sculls. She was on the heavyweight national team from 1983 to 1985 and is competing as a heavyweight for a berth on the 1988 Olympic team.

"In 1987," says Heather Hattin, "losing weight to go lightweight added stress to the training. So did raising money, although there is a sort of pride in not getting support, in doing everything yourself. But lightweights are seen as lower, not on par with heavyweights. At the Worlds, our medals were different than the heavyweight medals, and a lot smaller. I don't know if they make that differentiation on purpose. Is there a difference? Well, it's nice knowing you're the best in your division, but I suppose it would be nice to know you're the best of anyone out there."

Because of her smaller stature, Heather does not have the ambivalence of many of the bigger women. "In everyday situations, I'm only a bit bigger than the average population. I fit in. I know people are sometimes astonished when they find I row. They say, 'Oh you don't have any muscles at all.' It's sort of nice being able to fool people."

The discrimination she does encounter comes from within the rowing world. The administration initially told her that she wasn't allowed to try out for the 1988 Olympic team. "As a lightweight I feel at the top of the heap, while as a heavyweight I constantly feel that I have to prove myself so my size isn't used against me. I'm always on the line when I'm a heavyweight. I have thought many times — if only I had their body, how much faster I would go. I was a bit envious. But I'm glad in the end I'm the size I am. It's made me a real fighter, someone who has confidence in themselves to go out and get it no matter what someone else says." Her bottom line is performance, perhaps in a less complicated way than for the heavyweights, who have to deal with the size/femininity contradiction.

Heavyweight women aren't sure what they think of lightweights. Today's lightweight women rowers epitomize the late 1980s ideal of aerobically fit and successful women. As the newest class of entrants to the World Championships, they are bringing with them the bright, body-emphasizing fashion of aerobic wear. Rowing, easily the most conservative sport going, right down to its training garb, is adjusting. But only slowly. Both the men and women heavyweights have long worn tights, but they have been black and made of cotton or wool. The lightweight women get a lot of attention because of their looks. They have to put up with losing weight while trying to race, but society reinforces the dieting. Since they get unqualified approval, psychologically they have less trauma about their body image. But the criticism they face is that they are not as good athletes as the heavyweights. It's not quite fair, because they train hard and they row well. But as a group they aren't as fast, so they haven't been taken as seriously. It's a familiar story. It is the dilemma the Canadian heavyweight women face when they are compared with the men. Long on pink shirts, short on power.

For men, physical power and sex appeal — their version of pink shirts — go together. For women, power and sex appeal traditionally have not gone together at all. There was the assumption that female rowers were not sexy because they were large. That attitude has put oarswomen a little behind in the meat market. One oarswoman was devastated when she found out her foreign heart-throb thought she was too tall and intimidating. He liked lightweights better. Another queenly rower had an opposite problem. She grew tired of dealing with "wimpy men" who were awe-struck by her bearing. However, one can ask with justice — who would want to be ahead in the meat market anyway? And beyond the meat market approach to the opposite sex, which is offensive to all people involved anyway, size doesn't matter.

"Rowing is enough of an occupation that you end up thinking and talking about it a lot, as well as doing it, so the people you get along with the best will be those who also think about rowing, other things being equal," says one oarsman. Most oarsmen get along well with most oarswomen. On the whole, oarsmen respect and support the oarswomen as people for what they do. And they naturally go out with each other as frequently as any people who are brought into contact by common interests. Many marry each other — on the World rowing circuit there are international love affairs.

Doing competitive sport at a high level takes great passion, and the intensity of the focus often extends into other areas of the athlete's life. "Rowing is a very sensual thing to do because it takes so much physical effort," says Carol Love, who was on the 1976 Olympic team and now coaches in Peterborough, Ontario. "You're in such good shape and so aware of your body. So it's not surprising that people in it are very physical with each other."

"Our team had a birthday brunch in the spring of 1980," recounts Heather. "Some of the women poured over pictures from the 1979 Worlds, exclaiming about the best male bodies. They put in their bids for which guys they'd go after that year at the Olympics. I was shocked. With my evangelical upbringing I had never talked about sex like that. I didn't know the women well enough to know that it was just in fun."

Over the years, Heather learned that such joking was just part of the earthy rowing culture — no more and no less important than that. As long as athletes keep clear their priority of racing, and trust their crewmates to do so, whiling away an idle moment by being silly hurts no one.

In July 1986, some six years after that brunch in 1980, Heather was standing with the Canadian team, waiting to go into the stadium at the opening ceremonies of the Commonwealth Games in Edinburgh. All the countries' teams were standing in groups around a big grassy field. Just over from the Canadians were the Australians in their bright yellow blazers. The athletes, getting restive from standing for so long, started to chat, complain, look around. One of Heather's teammates asked her what she wanted for her birthday, since it was coming up.

"I said, 'Male, six four, dark curly hair, green eyes,'" reminisces Heather. "I thought it was a safe thing to say because I didn't think anyone on our team fit that description. Then someone pointed across the field at the Australian men's rowing team. 'There he is!' All the women got into the action, pointing and laughing at the Australian team. Sarah Ogilvie headed across the field — she's such a character, I knew she would fetch him. I was getting embarrassed. 'No, not that one,' I said. 'I like the guy with the straight hair better!' By this time all the Aussies were waving back and grinning. Fortunately for the maintenance of order, it had come time for the Canadian team to go into the stadium, so Sarah got back into formation.

"A week later, on my birthday, a group of us were flirting with Martin Cross, a Brit who is best buddies with all the Canadian women. Sarah suddenly started to whisper conspiratorially with him, and then she disappeared. She returned a few moments later with another strapping British fellow in tow, wearing Sarah's hair ribbon tied on his wrist in a bow. 'Happy birthday, Heather!' My present was sandy-haired, blue-eyed, freckled Adam Clift, not the dark god of my imaginings. But you don't look a gift horse in the mouth — even if he doesn't quite have the specified features. I got a birthday kiss."

Athletes know what their bodies can accomplish and take great pleasure in them. They do not have the inhibitions about physical expression that many non-athletes may have. Thus, at the party after the World Championships, people go wild. They spend the summer going to bed every night at ten, not drinking, and saving their legs for the next morning's workout. After the Worlds they revel in staying up all night, drinking and dancing the night away. Some people couple up as well, but how different is that from other people's wild parties?

"You're so disciplined most of the time, and so isolated in your training environment, that when you let loose, you go a bit crazy," explains Carol. "In 1976 the women had been training alone for a long time, and then we got together with the men and had a couple of incredible parties, where everyone went a bit wild. But is that being loose? I don't think so."

Athletes are unlike other people in that they learn to divorce their emotional response from physical sensation. Thus, an athlete will say, "My legs are telling me that they're tired." This separation allows them to push back their physical limits in sport.

The detachment of emotion from physical expression, while useful in sport, can limit a person's ability to achieve intimacy in a committed sexual relationship. But that is not at all the general rule. Some rowers do go through a promiscuous stage, but mostly because they are rowing at the age when they would be experimenting anyway. The majority grow out of it. And when they do settle down, most put a lot of effort into their commitments. They have learned in rowing how to work hard at things that matter to them.

Separation of their emotions from their physicality costs women more than it does men. Although views on sexual liberty are changing rapidly, the double standard regarding sexual behaviour still permits men to sow more wild oats. In 1987 a Canadian oarsman volunteered to Heather, "If the Canadian women would stop screwing around, they would get more results. The Canadian women are known as mattresses. I know. I'm living in Europe and I hear these things. Everyone knows the Canadian women for a good time. I'm just being frank."

False and irrelevant as the impression is, it goes one step further. A male coach who does not want to be named, said, outright, "Women are attracted to rowing because of the men." The men who row have beautiful bodies by any standard. They are also, according to the image, going to be successful later on in life. Therefore, if a woman's priority is to catch a good man then by that theory rowing is indeed a good place to look.

"Do women row because of the men?" asks Carol Love. "It's as stupid as asking if women go to law school or medical school because of the men." Carol married an oarsman on the '76 Olympic team. "If a woman goes out with a rower, she's accused of rowing because of the men. But if she goes out with a non-rower, he's seen as a bit of a wimp, as not cutting it." Why should oarswomen be damned if they do and damned if they don't?

"How can men say what women row for?" asks Kathy Lichty. "They don't know where women are coming from. Personally, I'm not concerned with what other people say anyway. Otherwise I wouldn't have done a lot of things I have. I don't go out and think about the guys and what they're doing. I just go out and think about myself and my crew."

Some women may *start* rowing for the men. But they don't last long. If they are only there for the men, they presumably worry what the men think. One man said that in his experience in university "some of the male students felt that it was unnatural for true women to compete physically at a high level. Lots of the women agreed with this argument at some level, or else feared that someone else agreed with it at some level, so they didn't try rowing as seriously as they might have otherwise, unlike many of the men. A lot of girls I knew tried rowing, then decided it would give them enormous shoulders and hips. They gave it up or else rowed intramurally. The women who were really into rowing did not let that deter them."

Rowing seriously takes too much effort to do it just for the men, and God knows there are easier ways to meet them! Strong and tall women who start rowing love the sport for what it does for them. It makes them proud of and comfortable in their bodies. As one woman said, "I finally realized what these legs were built for." Rowing is liberating.

"I want to be strong, lean and beautiful all at once," says Silken. Silken is pretty in a traditional way — she is blonde, blue-eyed and exhuberant. "There is no sacrifice," she states. "Being heavy is not bad."

In the final analysis, how the oarswomen feel about themselves is what they care about. They glory in being strong and healthy, in achieving through their own efforts. And if they ever feel a twinge — well, it doesn't last. As one woman says, "Sometimes when you see one of your old competitors who has whittled herself down to 120, you feel kind of awkward. You maybe try to justify in your mind — am I doing the right thing? But when you're rowing and training and just jogging along and you feel really good, you don't really care."

9

HAVING IT ALL

"One of my best friends in the Romanian pair was always aware when the Canadian pair was in her race!" Valeria, the former Romanian Olympic champion, speaks of the respect her teammate and fellow Olympic gold medallist has for her former competition, Tricia Smith and Betty Craig. Tricia and Betty were medal contenders at the boycotted 1980 Moscow Olympics, missed a gold medal in 1981 in the last stroke of the World Championship race, won bronzes in 1982 and 1983 at the Worlds, and won silver again in 1984. That year they were behind the Romanians. Tricia also won bronze medals in the eight in 1977 and 1978, and bronze medals in the four in 1985 and 1986. "Where you have a celebrity, people will flock," says Kay. "There are always people around Tricia and Betty."

Betty has since retired, but Tricia retains her status in the rowing world. In 1988 she is thirty-one years old and she is on her fourth Olympic team. She has travelled extensively and spent two seasons training in Italy. After an undergraduate degree in international relations, Tricia studied law at the University of British Columbia in her hometown of Vancouver. Because of her rowing, she did her law degree in an unorthodox way — by taking two spring terms off and by doing her bar admission exams before her articling at the Vancouver law firm of Alexander Holburn Beaudein & Lang in 1987. They hired her, knowing that she would take a substantial part of 1988 away from her work in order to compete at Seoul and at pre-Olympic regattas. Tricia has been able to maintain personal ties with her family and friends. If she didn't row, she would ski in the winter at her family's cabin at Whistler, outside of Vancouver. She lives in a basement apartment on the beach in trendy Kitsilano. Diplomatic and articulate, Tricia has been an advocate of athletes' rights. As such, she has been on the Canadian Olympic Committee's Athlete Advisory Council, and she has chaired the Rowing Athletes' Council.

"I think sometimes people look at a such a person and say — 'Hey, they've got it all. If I had their talent and my work ethic, I'd be even better,'" says Drew, who coached Tricia from 1984 to 1986. "People don't realize that the person who appears to have it all may have made enormous sacrifices and worked extraordinarily hard. They just make these easy assumptions. Tricia has enormous talent and she's worked really hard to develop it. She has done a very good job of managing her life. She's arranged it so as not to be taken away from her home all the time and yet she's been away an awful lot too. She's lucky now that she's been able to combine her professional life with her training. But people don't realize the turmoil she's had to go through, having to ask her employers if she can take off nearly half a year from her job. So having it all? That's an illusion." Tricia would be the first to agree.

From the outside, Tricia may look as though she has it all, since she has traditional success. But the reason she gives that strong impression of success is because she has confidence. She has rowed for so many years that she knows exactly what she needs to do to perform, and she has long since built a solid training base. Tricia has also thought out her priorities and knows the opportunity costs of what she does.

"You can't do everything 100 per cent all the time — you just run out of time," explains Tricia. "I think I just had to pace myself and decide year by year or month by month what my priority was, depending on the situation. I purposely put myself in training situations where I could stay in Vancouver — being able to do that has been one reason I have kept rowing. And I've had to juggle things and make sure I'm putting on the right emphasis. Rowing has been a priority over the years. Last year, though, I was articling and wanted to be hired back, so rowing had to be put on the back burner." The price Tricia paid for putting her work first was finishing eighth in the pair in 1987, but she kept her hand in for her long-term goal of the Olympics. "I knew it would be almost impossible to take 1987 off and be in there for 1988."

Only because 1988 is Tricia's fourth Olympic team could she consider taking a long-term look. Athletes who are not as established in the sport, or are not as talented, cannot take the same risks. To achieve her best, however, even she has to choose. "There is a conflict between keeping a balance and pursuing excellence, although it has been the balancing year by year that has enabled me to keep up this level of rowing for so long. For now, rowing is on the front burner."

Any athlete who tries to row and work full time has an insane schedule. Jane Tregunno and Kathryn Barr both tried to hold down full-time jobs in the winter of 1987-88. Kathryn, who is doing a master's degree at Western as well as training, took her job at a sports store in London only because she could not live on her carding cheque. Jane, who was taking courses part time, worked as a bank teller in Ottawa.

Cramming two workouts in around a job goes something like this. Getting up at 5:30 a.m. Working out from 6 to 8 a.m., then showering and snatching breakfast. Stuffing lunch, training clothes, baby powder, towels, T-shirts, running shoes into a bag, and rushing out the door. Both Kathryn and Jane stand on their feet all day at work and then stumble home to do a ninety-minute evening workout. They cannot eat for at least an hour after working out, as it takes their stomachs that long to settle down. Then they collapse into bed.

A full-time job drains athletes to the extent that even if they have the energy to fit in all their scheduled workouts, which they often do not, it can still prevent them from improving in their training. Rowers are unusual in that they can even *think* of holding jobs — unlike cyclists, for instance, who travel around the racing circuit for months on end. But within reason, rowers enjoy working hard and are ambitious in other areas besides their sport. And their willingness to take risks to do what they really want may be a great strength throughout their lives, if backed by the self-discipline used in sport.

"I want to make sure that my career will give me the same feeling as rowing," says Jane Tregunno, who is training to be an accountant and has a job waiting for her when she comes home from Seoul. "When I row, I feel like I'm on top of the world. Whatever anyone does doesn't faze me because I know I'm good at this and no one's going to knock me off that pedestal."

Following their hearts serves athletes well if they adapt their expectations to the circumstances of life after sport. But they can be left bemoaning their lost glory days if they fail to accept the realities of the sometimes more prosaic work world. Yes, there are the rowing groupies and the has-beens, who can't let go of their glory days. But most rowers adjust to the change. Without making too big a deal about it, they try to carry the lessons they learned from rowing into the rest of their lives.

Most rowers make the transition out of sport successfully. Of the athletes in sports that require strength and fitness, rowers are among the oldest, along with paddlers, marathoners and cross-country skiers. Having spent more time as adults working rowing into their lives, they have a realistic outlook on their situation. Moreover, since rowing lacks the financial rewards of other sports, rowers know from the start that they have to make a living elsewhere, unless they coach. In Canada there are very few professional coaching positions, and coaching is, in any case, a very demanding job. Coaches must put in incredible hours during the training season and spend a great deal of time on the road at regattas. They are judged by how well they produce in the very chancy world of racing. The pressure on their personal lives is great. Other rowers, who ultimately want to leave the sport, have a hard time balancing sport and career in the years of overlap. But having other fish to fry ultimately prevents the social dislocation that, say, a professional athlete could suffer on coming out of his or her sport. And since most rowers have never been celebrities, they don't miss the applause after they retire.

Rowers can still find themselves off balance when they retire. Socially, they can miss the close circle of the national team group. One problem with crew bonding is that it is so immediate, so here-and-now oriented, that people who leave can be forgotten — not as friends in the larger scheme, but as buddies. Rowers are swept up in the all-consuming round of training and racing, and just don't have the time to keep in touch. But when retired rowers do get back together with their old teammates, the barriers of time and different experience vanish. They enthusiastically relive the old days and tell their push-button stories of triumph and disaster one more time.

The usual pattern in sport is to think in four-year segments. As Tina says, tongue-in-cheek, "You have to quit after an Olympic year, don't you?" Families and non-rowing friends most often encourage athletes to move on around that watershed, since they see sport as play, albeit highly directed.

"My family is really supportive," says Jane Tregunno, "but by the 1984 Olympics I remember my brother saying to me, 'When are you going to get a real job and grow up?'" Because she was just twenty-two that year, the question did not bother her too much. But by the fall of 1985, with her B.Sc. at McMaster behind her, she did not know what to go on to. She had been considering retiring, but that seemed threatening. She knew she would miss the structure of the familiar lifestyle.

The structure of an athlete's schedule, while comforting in its familiarity, can be confining. "I needed more space to myself," says Barb Armbrust about taking the summer of 1987 off and rowing on her own in a single. Since 1980, when she was seventeen, she had rowed nationally every summer. "My views on issues were being heavily influenced by what I saw in the rowing world. Rowing is sheltered and stable. It's possible to get too used to it. Also, in many ways there is so much conformity, despite the fact that everyone has a strong character. It was good to take a breather."

"The difference in your life after you finish rowing is that suddenly nothing is planned. Before, when you row and go to school, you know when your training camps are, when your midterms are," says Jane. She looked high and low for something to do, feeling rootless and confused. Then in 1986, through the Olympic Career Centre in Toronto, which was set up for athletes in Jane's position, she found a goal again, this time in accounting.

"Accounting seemed like the perfect thing when it came along," says Jane, "because I could keep going in rowing but have something to go to and be accredited for by the end of 1988. I wasn't wasting my life." When athletes begin to hear that they should start real life, it makes them feel like they are just putting in time. They are all susceptible to the standards of the non-rowing world. They have to decide that for them it is legitimate to keep on. Athletes have different pressures on them, depending on their family background, gender, social and educational background, and previous success. Each athlete legitimizes a commitment to sport in a different way, according to his or her own expectations.

"The amount you have to legitimize staying in rowing is balanced by your success and what you're trying to do alongside it," says Doug Hamilton. Doug lives a version of success in line with the traditional elite image of rowing. Like Tricia, he is beginning his law career while rowing internationally. From the beginning, he has known what he wanted. In 1979 he became frustrated with crew rowing and learned how to scull in a single. In 1981 he tried and failed to make the national team, missing the time standard because of adverse wind conditions. In 1982 he lost the single trials race, so once again he missed the World Championships. Finally, in 1983 he made the national team quad. Since 1984, his crew has medalled every year at the

Worlds. In 1985 they bucked the system and won the gold. They trained together only on weekends for much of the summer. Because of their other commitments, they trained in singles and doubles the rest of the time. Their coach was dubious of this approach, and understandably, since most crews need time together to gel. But they were experienced oarsmen, and they clicked.

Because they were so successful, the system opened up for them when they pushed it. This allowed Doug to move to Britain in the fall of 1986 to do his master's in law at the London School of Economics. Since all the students had to write their final exam at exactly the same time, no matter where they were in the world, Doug wrote his the morning of his 1987 World Championship final. That afternoon he won a bronze medal in one of the best races of his life. He says, "It was a better race than in 1985 when we won the gold." All in a day's work. While training for the 1988 Olympics, Doug is teaching law at Queen's University in Kingston, Ontario. He has also been hired by a law firm in Toronto.

For any rower who wants that kind of success, Doug's choices, hard work and persistence serve as a model. But women have to travel a different path than men do towards success, whatever success they want. Men have more pressure sooner, perhaps, to start training for a career. Women have less pressure but they have more confusion — fewer clear role models. Also, no one quite knows how long in sport is "too long" for women, as it is a new environment for them.

"Male athletes are more valued by society than female athletes," Doug Hamilton observes. "Society perceives a difference between them. Female athletes who stay in sport for a long time are seen as wasting their time until they can find something better to do. I don't agree with the idea, but unfortunately our female athletes do little to discredit the image. Few female athletes further their careers while they row, while male athletes do much more. I know there are a lot of exceptions to both. But everyone should take the chance to get higher degrees, go to law school. We do get our tuition paid for. Instead, many of the women come out of rowing and go, 'What's next?'"

To support their rowing, many athletes hold a low-status, low-paying job. Their hard training and competitive schedule means that they usually delay entry into careers. Many more of the women have done this than the men, because more of the women have done rowing on their own steam.

"Why are all the women waitressing so that they can keep on rowing," asked Tina after the 1984 Olympics, "while the men are starting high-powered jobs?" Both the men and the women had the same academic credentials at that point — they were all finishing up B.A.'s and a few M.A.'s. Doug agrees that there is a difference. "A lot of the men come from private school backgrounds with correspondingly high expectations. A lot of the women don't."

Family background plays more of a part in rowers' choices than they always appreciate. But it is not the only thing that distinguishes the men rowers from the women rowers. Silken Laumann commented that "goal-orientation is more encouraged in all men from the start, getting patted on the back, for it helps them perform. Women don't get that. As well, less career opportunities exist for women, making everything that much more difficult. Women therefore have a harder road, and end up paying a higher price later for having rowed, as it shortens their careers that little bit more." Another athlete pointed out that, as well, "men don't have to decide they'll take a year off to have children." Now, when they are nearing thirty, the oarswomen feel the same pressures as other women their age — to have an established career and a first child. "The good thing about rowing though," says Silken idealistically, "is that when women athletes come out of sport, they'll be that much more ready to attack the world," presuming they had planned how they would go about it.

The older oarswomen have. Tina moved to Vancouver in 1985 so that she could get good rowing. In order to pay off her student loans from Princeton, she got a job at a delicatessen. By the end of her two years there, she was managing the place. In September 1987 Tina enrolled at UVic in preparatory courses for a master's in public administration. Going to school in Victoria fit better with pre-Olympic training than working, and Tina in any case wants to do a business-related master's degree before she starts her own business. Lisa has finished qualifying as a teacher of English as a second language. As she trains for 1988, she is teaching a few hours a week and loving it. Andrea is finishing her master's in physiology at a lab connected with her training site in Italy, and wants to go on to do a Ph.D. Kay is not quite sure yet what she will do.

"Keeping on rowing has meant I've been involved in physical fitness longer," says Kay. "Probably lifelong now. Maybe I've already made a career decision different than it would have been had I not stayed in rowing. In my coaching job at the University of Pennsylvania I see a lot of women coming into rowing at eighteen or so, with no awareness of their bodies, of fitness, or of life. And also, a lot of women have injuries at eighteen that will be lifelong — knee or back — that they have because of stupidity, because of lack of information on behalf of coaches who believed in 'beat your head against the wall till you drop' training, 'cause otherwise they wouldn't be training hard enough. I can do something to repair that."

Some oarswomen have chosen a traditional male version of success. Getting on the male track poses the same difficulties for oarswomen as for all women — they have to search for their role models. Tricia, as we know already, has chosen law. Anne Marden, the American single sculler, who is in her third Olympic year in 1988, figured out how to row and pursue a career on the scale of Doug Hamilton's legal career. But it took her some time. After graduating from Princeton in 1981, she took a job at a sport store so she could keep training. She justified her decision to stay in sport well after college by winning a silver in the U.S. quad in 1984, but only after a few dry years when people wondered what she was up to. She started her M.B.A. in January 1985, and things began to fall into place. She kept on rowing, partly because she could go to a lot of good races easily. "In 1985, when I was in business school in France, I wanted to go to Lucerne and race the single. But to get funding, you had to win the single trials, and I never had. Then one day I realized — 'I don't have to win the single trials to go to Lucerne, all I have to do is go! I'm already in France.' But I went back home to the U.S. and won the single trials anyway and got sent. Why do we have this feeling that you can only do what you're told you can do or should do? There are things out there that you can do, if you've got the resources. All you have to do is go." That doesn't hold true for all races. While anyone can go to summer regattas on their own, athletes are sent by their country to the Worlds and therefore must qualify by jumping through the proper hoops. At the Worlds Anne won a bronze medal in the single in 1985, and a bronze in the double in 1987.

In 1986 Anne landed a job with the J.P. Morgan Investment Company. She warned all the firms that interviewed her that she wanted to work only thirty-five hours a week. The J.P. Morgan Company knew what athletes' schedules were like, having had runner Mary Decker on staff, so it supported Anne's rowing. The company hired and paid Anne in London, England, and allowed her the four to five weeks of holiday that she needed for competition. And rowing has helped Anne out professionally — to her surprise another company asked her to join the president at a big lunch one day because his daughter had just started rowing at school. Once Anne had figured out her career plan and priorities, she saw where she could bend her rowing and work situations to suit her needs. It is never easy and it takes all her time, but the rewards are great.

"Doing this in a way alienates you from your other teammates, though," says Anne, "because you set your sights above and beyond them, not so much in terms of competition, but in terms of what you'll do to get there. I don't know many athletes who would go to a bank and borrow $10,000 to spend on rowing for the summer. That's what you have to be willing to do." When a top athlete takes control and turns the system to his or her own advantage, everyone else is by implication issued a challenge to do so too. It can be hard on other athletes who would do the same thing if they could, but are simply not in as strong a position. For the person who does try, it means being willing to take risks, and be disapproved of. But it also may be the only way that such a person is willing to continue.

"Rowing in the pair gave me the opportunity to have control of my own life," says Tricia. "That's been key to why I've been able to stay in rowing for so long. If I didn't fit into a particular plan, I could work something out and still reach my full potential. I could work in an environment and with the people that suited me and my situation. I find that my frame of mind is really, really important. I like to have some input. If I'm in a situation where I have confidence, I'll happily keep on working as hard as I can."

"The system is based on optimizing athletes' performances and at the same time take into consideration the athletes' other commitments — maybe school or work," says Jim Joy. Although it tries, the system doesn't always live up to its aims, as Kay found out after she won the 1987 single trials and tried to stay in Philadelphia. Tricia and Betty managed to make the system accommodate them when they were in the pair, but the circumstances were different. For one thing, their success was more established than Kay's, and for another, the system was less developed.

"We decided in the spring of 1982 that going to Italy would be a good way of continuing in rowing but maintaining our enthusiasm," says Tricia. "Our decision had a lot to do with the fact that our coach was in Italy and we saw no one else in Canada who could help us achieve our level." The Canadian system is oriented around camps, where the whole team trains together and the coach chooses the crews. Selecting all the boats from a pool of athletes makes for the most possible combinations. With a camp system, a small country like Canada makes the most of its people. But such a system may limit the power of individual athletes to choose what they want to do. And sometimes the system cannot take top athletes to their peak performance. In the case of Tricia and Betty, taking the step of going off to train in Italy, especially with a coach who had left his position in Canada, was unprecedented, and they were told as much. "We were given a rough time about leaving the Canadian system, and then when we mentioned that we were given a rough time, we were given a rough time about that. But maybe it's a function of being in a small boat and apart from the general picture. People don't always understand exactly what you're doing, and when people don't know what's going on, they imagine things are going on which really aren't. It's just communication. It's human dynamics."

Taking responsibility for one's own life is a concept that is foreign to the traditional female. Women who hope to have marriage and a family often still expect to plan their own lives around the needs of others. Women often subordinate their other goals to the goal of having a relationship. A younger athlete on the team says, "In a relationship, it's the girl who's more willing to sacrifice her time to be with the guy, while for him, rowing comes first." That may be true for certain individuals at certain times in their careers, but for the women on the 1988 team, rowing is high on the list of priorities for now. The women are not, at least in the short run, subordinating their own goals in rowing to their ties with men.

For Angie, it is either rowing or a serious relationship. In 1984, she felt that there was nothing for her, in terms of emotional commitment, outside the members of the four — Jane, Marilyn, Barb, Angie and Lesley. "Jane was going out with the stroke seat of the men's eight — but it wasn't a consuming relationship on either side, because he was so focused on his rowing too. Marilyn was engaged to be married in September 1984 to a rower. But he was 3,000 miles away when we were training. Marilyn would talk about him incessantly, but she was never with him." It is Angie's considered opinion that, for her, Olympic-level rowing and a committed relationship are incompatible: "People who deny that may have a relationship where that person is the first other *person* in their life, but still rowing's ahead of the relationship.

"In the fall of 1984 I wanted to go through to the '88 Olympics and win a gold medal. And then I met Robert. And that was the very first time since I started rowing that I met someone who was more important to me than rowing was. I tried to pretend to myself that I took 1985 off only because of my herniated disc, but there was no question that it was Robert. If it weren't for Robert, I actually think I would have rowed until I was crippled. But I yearned for rowing. I started training in the fall of 1985, and then I herniated my disc again. Total devastation, because I'd never really admitted that I wanted to quit. I kept on, in spite of my injury. I really wanted Robert to see what had been the most important thing in my life before he met me. Also, I wanted to go to the Commonwealth Games and the World Championships because they were in England. Robert's family lives in England.

"That year, 1986, was one of the worst experiences I ever had. I was unprepared for it, physically and mentally. I was going to try to balance my relationship with Robert and rowing. Robert was a complete obsession. In 1984 there was nothing outside our crew. But in 1986, when we had time off, I would take a bus and go down to be with his family and pretend everything was normal. It was very traumatic. I just couldn't juggle rowing and Robert. I don't think it's possible to have it all. If you are satisfied with a relationship where you lead two individual lives and then meet sometimes — well, that can be perfectly happy and healthy, I suppose. But I'm so intense, I wanted us to be inseparable. To have that and rowing? Hah! It was a joke."

"Rowing has to be number one priority. It cannot include moderation," says Silken. "That does not fit with the image of the self-sacrificing woman. Self-sacrifice is a typical female quality. This gender stereotyping can induce guilt in women athletes." At different times in their lives, some athletes have found rowing and a relationship to be mutually exclusive. During the

World Championships one year, after being in Europe all summer competing, one oarswoman received a letter from her fiancé. He asked her to choose between himself and rowing. She chose rowing. Later she found a rower "who will let me do anything I want." Still, she has now retired from rowing. Most athletes find someone who will not ask them to make that choice.

Heather has changed her position on the issue. When she started on the national team, she thought she would never want to go out with a rower. She also thought that it was an either/or issue, and since she didn't have time or energy to divide herself between two passions, she chose rowing. But that couldn't work over the long run, which has turned out to be a decade. After her first summer on the team, she re-evaluated her position, having met a rower she wanted to go out with. Later, she reached the point where she looked *only* to rowers for relationships.

When rowing is everything, to go out with someone who doesn't row seems almost sacrilegious. Heather explains: "If you eat, breathe and sleep rowing, non-rowers could understandably be jealous of the commitment, or not understand it and be hurt. The difficulty in going out with a rower is that they have to maintain their focus too, and they may need a lot of support when you might not be able to provide it, or demand of you when you can't spare the energy to give." Thinking either "I can't have a relationship at all" or "I can't go out with someone who isn't a rower" is extreme. But rowers tend to be extreme. Says Heather, "I've lost myself in rowing, and in a relationship, because of my tendency to get so involved in what I do. Now that I'm thirty, I look at my relationship as a supportive platform, from which I am encouraged to be creative and to meet challenges. I expect to be nurtured, as well as nurturing. It is not my role as a woman to take on all the responsibility of a relationship. And I expect my partner to respect my pursuit of excellence, as I respect his priorities."

But such a relationship is very much one of our generation. Heather recently told her father of her plans "to row until 1988, and to do a professional degree. He asked if I had decided against marriage and children. When I asked him what he meant, he told me he worried that I wouldn't be normal — that men would be intimidated by me. I told him that if a man is intimidated by me doing my best at something, then I am not going to be interested in him anyway. I was surprised because he raised me with the idea that I should use the talents God gave me. It was ironic, though. My choice to get a professional degree was prompted by my desire to have it all. Although I have to admit I'm pretty idealistic too. I wanted the autonomy and the flexibility so that I *could* have marriage and children together with a satisfying career." Heather's version of having it all is to keep alive the nurturing, traditionally feminine aspect of her character, as well as be goal oriented. Her ultimate goal is wholeness of self, which is a highly subjective version of having it all, but probably the most enduring one. Whichever path she chooses, she will obviously pay the costs of not having taken the other option. But being a heroine is making one's own way in full awareness of the price.

Rowers get close to "having it all" because they are an extraordinarily fortunate group of people. They work hard and take risks, but they are assisted in myriad little ways by the people around them. "I would never have been able to do what I have done if it weren't for the support system around rowing," says Heather. "If it wasn't for coaches like Doug Clark in Woodstock who gave me the dream in the first place, or Ian McFarlane in Kingston, who volunteers all his time. Or John Armitage, who keeps Kingston Rowing Club going and co-signed the loan for my single. Or for the town of Woodstock, which got out and raised several thousand dollars for Tina and me and Stephen Beatty for the '84 Olympics. Or for my parents, who encouraged me, my older sisters, who had the courage to go out and do non-traditional careers and were my role models. Or for the people in St. Catharines, London and Victoria who put all the rowers up for the summers we trained there." The reality of high-performance sport in Canada is that athletes often feel that they are on the receiving end. It is hard on their pride to be financially dependent. Athletes' gifts in return are less tangible.

"Why would I quit rowing?" asks Kay. "Being twenty-eight and having too many things going by me. You look around and the societal norms say, 'Rowing? Why are you still doing that?' If expectations were different, the pressure to retire would be different." Mature athletes see their peers settling down into jobs, building houses and long-term relationships. Drew Harrison thinks that, despite the cost, "staying in sport is very worthwhile for mature athletes. Since they peak physiologically in their late twenties, they are pushing the limits of mankind's physical capabilities. That's an extraordinarily worthwhile thing to do. Still, I hope people recognize that rowing is not the be-all and end-all of life. In a short-term sense it may seem like that, but most are aware that this is a segment of life."

Many national team athletes see that there is life after rowing, but don't want to wait for it until then. When they think about life in the abstract, it seems like having it all is tough but not impossible. After winning an important race on a sunny summer afternoon, the rest of life seems relatively easy. Of course rowing will always be the priority! Halfway through a winter of trying to train and work, though, many rowers are exhausted. National team rowers are high achievers. As a group, they tend to become compulsive overachievers if they don't watch out. As Silken, who is known for her enthusiasm about every project she takes on, says, "I run myself down. I suffer a lot of mental conflict and constantly play little games with myself — that is, if I put more here, would that suffer? On the bottom line, though, having it all is an attitude. You want to enjoy life." Lisa Robertson does enjoy life. She states firmly that "I reserve my intensity for rowing alone, and I pursue other things in a more relaxed way." By nature relaxed, she says, "The change in me due to rowing is in how I approach things that I *really* want. I now know how to compete with myself, and that I have a certain stubbornness which helps me achieve my goals."

The realistic attitude these mature athletes have means that most of them will be able to walk away from rowing when the time comes. For the time being, they have committed themselves through to the beginning of October 1988, which is the end of the Seoul Olympics. They will put rowing on the front burner until then. After Seoul, many who are considering retirement will play the situation by ear. "If we do really well at Seoul and I decide to return to school and can fit rowing into my schedule," says Heather, "then I may keep going. I'm at my physiological peak. I still have a few years left in me."

Tricia applies the goal orientation that rowing taught her to her career. "Sport gave me the confidence that I can tackle anything. I know that I can just break the task down and go after it step by step. When I encounter a problem, I know I can surmount it. When I have something to do, I think, 'Of course I can do it.' I guess if you can get through the pain of a 2,000-metre race, you can get through anything. It seems silly because rowing seems to be totally physical, and practising law obviously is different. But any performance in rowing has been worked over piece by piece. You use imagery in rowing, and you can use imagery in law too. You imagine different scenarios and how you will deal with them. You can apply the principles of sport to anything, including something that's more cerebral."

Kay agrees with Tricia. "In rowing you can set goals for yourself and strive to achieve them. You get lots of satisfaction and it's a great confidence builder in that way. A friend of mine on the team from 1982 to 1984 said, 'Rowing didn't help me get a job, but having spent so much time racing and in the weight room learning to interrelate on a basic level and be tough, has really helped me. The business world is male dominated. But I had learned how to be tough through rowing, and the men who tried to intimidate me in the field of sales just couldn't do so. I've achieved more in the work world than other women who came in before me.'" By some definitions used in the "real world," Kay does not yet know what she will do "when she grows up." But she has learned what the school of hard knocks has to teach

— realism. "How to be smart and not knock your head against the wall unnecessarily. Rowing taught me how to be persistent in hard times, to keep plugging. And that I'm strong-minded but I'm not belligerent. Realizing how to play the game and when to toe the line or stand up for yourself is important."

CONCLUSION

The women on the Canadian Olympic rowing team are committing their utmost to preparation for Seoul. They are focused on the goal of a medal. Day by day they train intensely and anticipate the final Olympic race. On the day of that final race, all the life experience, all the training and all the races that have gone in to preparing them will be as nothing, because victory or defeat comes down to the six and a half minutes in the boat. In 1988 the strongest medal contenders are the eight and the single — the boats given priority for this Olympics. All of the oarswomen know that it will take the coincidence of top-notch athletes meshing perfectly, pulling together for themselves and each other.

But after the racing is over, the athletes will remember all the richness of their experience in sport. They will remember the funny things that happened, the calamities they endured and the friends they made, as well as the great races they rowed. Even now when they look back over the years — and on average the older oarswomen in 1988 have rowed for a decade — they see the effect that rowing has had on them, how they have been socialized as athletes.

"Evaluation has become a really natural thing for us," says Lisa. "For example, when Tina started working out at Nautilus Fitness Centre last year, she had a fitness test because they wanted to evaluate her. The tester was really impressed with how fit she was, but also how calm she was. He said, 'People come in and they're nervous wrecks about it.' Tina said, 'Of course I'm calm, we do this all the time. We're so used to it.' We *are* used to evaluating, criticizing ourselves. I know that will stand us in good stead later on — being able to accept that and use it

positively. Rowing also showed me you can take any situation
and turn it around and make it work positively. Heather and I in
the double in 1986 were a good example. I don't know if I would
have learned to work things out so well without having rowed."

Rowing has made the women comfortable with being big,
being strong and being physical, with defining their place in a
non-traditional environment for women, with letting go and
having fun. The down side is that rowing can encourage inappropriate or disproportionate responses outside its confines. But
for most, rowing has been a positive and formative influence. In
it, they grew from being idealistic teenagers to adults with the
confidence to realize their dreams.

"What I like about rowing changes depending on my mood,"
says Kay. "Sometimes it's being up in the early morning, before
everyone else, on the crisp clear river. And sometimes it's when
the boat's going particularly well. Sometimes it's the
camaraderie. Or the sheer fitness — having a really good piece
and being totally wasted from it. For me it changes with the time
of year and the type of training. It's a way of learning about
yourself — pushing to your limit."

In deciding to compete at the Olympics, athletes set their
wills to get what they want. In the process, they learn to define
their priorities clearly. They learn to be strong, to put up with
situations, to make friends, to get along with people when they
need to. They shape their lives by choosing to focus on training.
On the road to the Olympics, the decision to go forward must be
reconfirmed every day. Athletes need to push back the limits of
their bodies' abilities in each training session, so they can improve.

The physical and psychological are inextricably bound. The
athlete must believe she can achieve her goals. "In 1987 I
thought about winning a gold medal all summer," says Heather
Hattin, who won in the lightweight doubles at the Worlds with
partner Janice Mason. "How great it would be. Whenever I im-
agined we had won or were standing on the podium, I would get
a jolt all through my body. After we won our heat we had to wait

five days for our final. That was probably the longest five days
I've lived. By the time the race day came, I just wanted to get it
over with, I'd been thinking about it so much. Actually winning
the gold medal was almost anti-climactic. I didn't expect that we
would win, but I knew we could. If we hadn't won, I would have
been really disappointed. It's so satisfying to have a goal and
then go through all the hassles to get there and then actually
achieve that goal."

These oarswomen are tough, determined and goal oriented.
They are also romantics of a high order. They row because they
love it for its own sake. They connect to rowing not only because it is competition, but also because in rowing they connect
to other people and to themselves. Rowing is a celebration of
their talents and their persistence. One athlete says that she continues in sport because where she trains "there are children at the
club. When you go there and see little girls running around gig-
gling, it makes you appreciate sport. You're not out there just to
beat the East Germans, you're out there to watch somebody grow
up and have fun."